Comprehensive Tax Reform

The Colombian Experience

**Edited by Parthasarathi Shome, with
contributions from David Dunn, Erik Haindl,
Arnold C. Harberger, and Osvaldo Schenone**

INTERNATIONAL MONETARY FUND
Washington DC
March 1995

Library of Congress Cataloging-in-Publication Data

Comprehensive tax reform : the Colombian experience / edited by
Parthasarathi Shome.
     p.   cm. — (Occasional Papers, ISSN 1251-6365 ; 123)
    Includes bibliographical references.
    ISBN 1-55775-430-6
    1. Taxation—Colombia. I. Shome, Parthasarathi, 1950– .
II. Series: Occasional paper (International Monetary Fund) ; no. 123.
HJ2545.C66   1995
336.2'05'09861—dc20   95-6823
                                            CIP

Price: US$15.00
(US$12.00 to full-time faculty members and
students at universities and colleges)

Please send orders to:
International Monetary Fund, Publication Services
700 19th Street, N.W., Washington, D.C. 20431, U.S.A.
Tel.: (202) 623-7430   Telefax: (202) 623-7201
Internet: publications@imf.org

recycled paper

Contents

Page

Page

Charts

Section

The following symbols have been used throughout this paper:

. . . to indicate that data are not available;

— to indicate that the figure is zero or less than half the final digit shown, or that the item does not exist;

– between years or months (e.g., 1991–92 or January–June) to indicate the years or months covered, including the beginning and ending years or months;

/ between years (e.g., 1991/92) to indicate a crop or fiscal (financial) year.

"Billion" means a thousand million.

Minor discrepancies between constituent figures and totals are due to rounding.

The term "country," as used in this paper, does not in all cases refer to a territorial entity that is a state as understood by international law and practice; the term also covers some territorial entities that are not states, but for which statistical data are maintained and provided internationally on a separate and independent basis.

Preface

During 1991–94, the Colombian authorities requested the Fund's Fiscal Affairs Department (FAD) for technical assistance in their ongoing tax reform. In support of their effort, four studies were undertaken in selected areas of tax policy and administration. These efforts were headed by the editor, who is Chief of the Tax Policy Division of FAD. Other participants in the tax policy area included David Dunn, Economist, FAD, as well as members of the FAD panel of fiscal experts: Erik Haindl, Professor, University of Gabriela Mistral, Santiago de Chile; Arnold C. Harberger, Professor, University of California at Los Angeles; and Osvaldo Schenone, Professor, University of San Andres, Buenos Aires.

The investigations in the above-mentioned tax policy area, conducted in cooperation with the staff of the National Directorate of Taxes and Customs (DIAN), focused on particular areas that the authorities felt needed technical examination and recommendations. The investigations of issues under the value-added tax, income taxes, and customs tariffs thus constituted an examination of the major sources of tax revenue. Given the predominantly technical nature of the analyses and the broad scope of the studies, which touched upon comprehensive tax reform aspects, the authorities encouraged their publication for a wider readership.

This Fund Occasional Paper should therefore serve the dual purpose of elaborating on the technical intricacies behind the undertaking of tax structure reform and providing a representative example of the variety of studies undertaken by FAD in the provision of technical advice to member countries.

A number of background points should be underlined in connection with this study. First, in many ways, the various authors made important contributions to all the topics covered. Therefore, the assignment of particular authors to different sections (as noted at the beginning of each section) reflects the principal author who was clearly distinguishable. David Dunn was responsible for the analysis of potential income tax revenue in the section on income tax issues; Erik Haindl for the study in the same section of the impact of the income tax on investment; Arnold C. Harberger for the section on conclusions and future directions for tax reform (while also collaborating on selected aspects of the section on the value-added tax); and Osvaldo Schenone for the section on the customs tariff reform and the analysis of inflation adjustment in the income tax issues section. The editor was responsible for the introduction, as well as the section on value-added tax issues, while holding overall responsibility as team leader.

Second, the two driving forces behind the endeavor were Mr. Rudolf Hommes, Minister of Finance and Public Credit, who initiated the requests and during whose tenure the visits covering the various topics took place, and Mr. Vito Tanzi, Director, Fiscal Affairs Department, who encouraged and approved their undertaking. Third, the study could not have been completed successfully in the absence of open discussions and full cooperation (including the provision of data) by the staff of the DIAN, in particular, the staff of the Center for Fiscal Studies of the DIAN. Fourth, detailed comments received from the many colleagues who advised the authors on earlier drafts were important in formulating the final version. They include Milka Casanegra-Jantscher, Isaias Coelho, Julio Escolano, Mario Garza, José Gil-Diaz, Jonathan Levin, Claire Liuksila, George Mackenzie, Paulo Neuhaus, Lorenzo Perez, Fred Ribe, and

Vito Tanzi. The assistance of Asegedech Woldemariam and Emmanuel Hife in producing Tables 1 and 37–38, respectively, is gratefully acknowledged. The editorial assistance of Tom Walter of the External Relations Department was extremely helpful. Of course, the responsibility of remaining errors remains with the various authors.

1 Introduction

A Latin American Perspective

At the beginning of the 1980s, most Latin American tax structures were complex and cumbersome. Often they were loaded with hundreds of taxes, with little revenue collected from most of them. Consumption and production taxes suffered from multiple rates, leading to difficulties with tax administration. These taxes were inefficient because of "cascading," that is, they fell not only on the value of production but also on taxes that had been paid in earlier stages of production, and they tended to impair international competitiveness because they were often levied at the manufacturing—rather than the retail—stage, so that exporters also effectively paid the tax. Income taxes were riddled with multiple exemptions and incentives and high rates, and suffered from a failure to integrate the taxing of personal and corporate incomes and a lack of indexation. These conditions led generally to low revenue productivity, inequities reflecting narrow tax bases, and inefficiencies in resource allocation, including biases in the debt-equity composition of business financing. On the whole, tax systems had to depend for revenue on a few highly distortive domestic taxes or on international trade taxes—including export duties.

The tax reforms that followed comprised either a series of steps taken over a significant number of years, as in Colombia (the "incremental" approach), or almost a sea change in policy, as in Argentina (the "revolutionary" approach). In general, the incremental approach prevailed, as the common experience was one of continuous formulation of reform policies and their steady, sequenced application. Reform-minded countries attempted to simplify their tax structures, focusing in the early years of the reform process on income taxation but moving over time toward the taxation of production and consumption. As the economies matured and became more integrated with the rest of the world, such as that of Mexico, the focus reverted to fine-tuning those aspects of the income tax that had international ramifications.

A cross-country comparison reveals that most countries that carried out tax reforms with the stated objectives of improving the efficiency, equity, neutrality, and administrative feasibility (simplicity) of their tax systems also experienced a perceptible increase in tax revenue-GDP ratios of 2–4 percent. Increases occurred regardless of whether, at the start of the reform, countries had low or high ratios of tax revenue to GDP (see Shome (1992)). This is understandable as a typical preoccupation of authorities undertaking reform was a downward slide in tax revenue, which they attributed to the prevailing cumbersome tax structure that they wished to correct. Thus, even though tax reforms need not necessarily be linked to revenue increases, this seems to have been invariably the case.

Countries with initial low ratios of tax revenue to GDP might continue to have rather low ratios, compared with other countries, after completing the reforms; however, their own ratios would increase. Thus, throughout the 1980s, most Latin American countries experienced significant increases in their tax revenue-GDP ratios pari passu with wide-ranging tax reforms—a trend that seems to have continued into the early 1990s.[1] However, the high expectations regarding continuing increases in tax revenue-GDP ratios should be contained, which also points toward the need for consistent efforts to curtail public expenditures for achieving fiscal balance.

History of Colombian Tax Reform

Tax reform in Colombia has resulted from many special commissions set up to examine broad or particular aspects of the tax system. The prospect of working with Colombia's highly qualified tax professionals, as well as the authorities' open welcome for a cross-fertilization of ideas, generated much interest in international tax experts, and many commission reports were submitted to the Government.[2]

Note: This section was prepared by Parthasarathi Shome.

[1]A few countries, such as Peru, stand out as exceptions. Nevertheless, even these countries started to make strong revenue efforts in the 1990s.

[2]For evaluations, see Musgrave and Gillis (1971), and Tanzi (1972); for descriptions, see McLure (1988).

Table I. Total Tax Revenue
(In percent of GDP; period average)

	1980–83	1984–87	1988–91	1992–94[1]
Operations of the central government[2]	10.14	11.33	12.62	16.29
Operation of the central administration	7.68	8.93	9.91	11.92
Net income and profits	2.89	3.27	4.18	5.17
Goods and services	2.78	3.30	3.61	5.45
General sales/value–added tax	1.97	...	2.91	4.70
Gasoline tax	0.81	...	0.70	0.74
International trade	1.74	2.01	1.92	1.21
Imports tariffs and surcharges	1.41	...	1.85	1.21
Coffee exports	0.33	...	0.08	—
Stamp and other taxes	0.28	0.35	0.19	0.10
Social security contribution	1.75	1.76	2.04	3.59
National decentralized agencies	0.71	0.65	0.68	0.79
Operations of local nonfinancial public sector	2.09	2.37	2.56	2.68
Operations of the general government[3]	12.23	13.70	15.18	18.97

Sources: Bank of the Republic; Ministry of Finance; National Planning Department; and IMF staff estimates.
[1]Preliminary figures for 1994.
[2]Includes central administration, social security, and national decentralized agencies.
[3]Includes central government and local nonfinancial public sector.

Thus, Colombia has been involved in a continuous tax reform effort over the decades, with each reform comprising an improvement of the existing tax structure. The reforms have involved both domestic taxes and taxes on international trade and have resulted, over the 1980–92 period, in a steady and significant increase equivalent to over 4 percent of GDP in the tax revenue of the central administration, which is the focus of this study (Table 1).

Colombia was one of the first Latin American countries to develop a consumption tax based on value added. Following its introduction in a rudimentary form in 1965, the reforms of 1968, 1971, 1974, 1983, 1986, and 1990 brought about various changes in the tax. However, one important feature of the consumption-type value-added tax (VAT) was missing: complete credit for taxes paid on purchases of capital goods. This feature was effectively introduced only in 1992, and even then as a credit against the income tax rather than against the VAT paid on sales.

With respect to income taxes, Colombia experienced two important reforms within the past ten years, in 1986 and 1990. Both reforms were designed to prevent double taxation of enterprises and individuals and to remove obstacles to investment. Interestingly, according to McLure (1988), Colombia had been also the first nation in the Western Hemisphere to impose an income tax, dating from 1821. A sched-

ular income tax was in effect for over a century, until it was changed to a global income tax in 1927.

The tax reform in recent years has also included customs tariff reform, which reduced the level of tariff rates from an average of 61 percent to 30 percent by 1986. However, a flat, across-the-board surcharge of 10 percent was introduced in 1985 and increased to 18 percent in 1987. These reforms coexisted with several quantitative restrictions on selected imports, and with selective export promotion schemes of varying effectiveness, which the authorities had been implementing since the late 1960s. By 1990, the need for a full-fledged trade liberalization was widely recognized; a program to that effect was implemented, whose pace was accelerated in 1991.

Objectives and Main Measures of Tax Reforms

Focusing only on the period beginning in 1980, the stated objective of the 1983 reform—the first major tax reform of the 1980s—was to encourage economic activity (as in the case of the 1984 Chilean reform) by reducing double taxation and increasing tax incentives. Measures actually taken included wide-ranging improvements in various taxes aimed at correcting some of the structural deficiencies of the prevailing tax system. The personal income tax structure underwent changes, such as a reduction in tax rates, for the purpose of promoting private sector economic activity. At this time, the personal exemption level was also increased, and the number of taxpayers was reduced. Meanwhile, other changes were introduced to facilitate tax administration, monetary correction for financial incomes of individuals, and presumptive taxation for commerce and financial intermediation. The tax rate for limited companies was reduced (multiple corporate income tax rates had prevailed), and double taxation was eliminated, although incentives of various sorts were granted. The base of the income-type VAT was extended to include several previously exempted services.

The 1986 Colombian tax reform attempted to achieve greater neutrality and equity, especially by restructuring the income tax and improving tax administration. Individual income tax rates were further reduced, 90 percent of salary earners began to pay tax through retentions only, corporate income tax rates were unified, and attempts were made to correct any continuing biases in the debt-equity ratios of companies caused by the tax system. On the administrative side, the reform simplified tax declaration forms, introduced tax payments through banks—thereby releasing many tax officials for other functions—and created large-taxpayer units.

The 1990 tax policy changes were carried out in the context of economic restructuring and modernization. They were focused on encouraging savings and improving the capital market through, among other measures, the encouragement of repatriation of capital and the opening of the economy through customs tariff reform. Therefore, in addition to reducing the corporate income tax rate, the authorities introduced a much lower tax rate for income from repatriated capital, exempted stock market income from taxation, and halved the withholding tax rate on repatriated income from foreign capital. The VAT rate was unified at 12 percent, and its base was further expanded. The import surcharge applicable on all imports was reduced to 13 percent (and eventually to 8 percent in 1994) while the average tariff was reduced from 16 percent to 7 percent. In the area of administration, a national directorate for taxes was created, with the objective of consolidating tax evasion strategies. This measure was complemented by a further drastic reduction in the number of taxpayers required to file declarations.

Tax policy changes continued in 1992–93 with the objective of lowering the fiscal deficit in the face of an inflation rate that hovered stubbornly near 30 percent. Increases in selected tax rates were accompanied by a sustained expansion of the tax base. Thus, an income tax surcharge was introduced to fund national security expenditures. Public and mixed enterprises, public funds, and financial cooperatives became taxable. However, the withholding tax on foreign remittances was reduced. The VAT rate was increased to 14 percent for five years, its base was broadened, and it was effectively converted to a consumption-type VAT to reduce cascading. Import restrictions were virtually eliminated. On the administrative side, domestic taxes and customs were consolidated into one directorate, with the intention of improving cross-controls and facilitating antievasion measures.

Thus, the Colombian tax policy changes could be said to have been of an incremental nature. The authorities' objectives have included a combination of particular short-run goals, such as encouraging savings, investment, and capital inflow, and medium-run goals, such as removing distortions, improving equity, and simplifying the tax system.[3] There may have been no revolutionary change, such as occurred in Argentina or even Bolivia, as the style selected was one of utilizing a wide scope of tax policy mixes. Colombia's use of the VAT has been somewhat less than Argentina's or Chile's, and its use of the income tax instrument is more comparable to Mexico's than those two countries. As in many Latin American countries during the period—as indicated previously—the tax policy changes in Colombia progressively increased the tax revenue-GDP ratio.

As a result of these reforms, the current tax system at the federal level comprises essentially six broad categories of taxes: taxes on income and profits, social security contributions, payroll taxes, taxes on goods and services, taxes on international trade, and stamp taxes. A description of these categories is provided in Appendix I.

The objective of this paper is to analyze particular areas of tax policy that have concerned the Colombian authorities during the 1990s, albeit comprising a comprehensive approach to tax reform over time. It is intended to allow the reader to view in technical detail the type of analysis conducted in a representative tax reform study carried out by the IMF.[4] The areas covered comprise (1) selected structural aspects and revenue potential of the VAT, which are discussed in Section II; (2) the impact of income tax on investment and revenue and inflation adjustment potentials, which is considered in Section III; (3) the customs tariff reform of 1992—including its revenue consequences and some alternative reform packages—which is explained in Section IV; and (4) the direction of future reforms, which is addressed in Section V.

---

[3]For further elaboration on the ramifications of tax reform, see Sanchez Torres and Gutiérrez Sourdis (1994).

[4]For surveys of the Fund's role in tax reform, see IMF (1993) and Tanzi (1994).

II Value-Added Tax Issues

Structural Aspects

As noted in Section I, Colombia was one of the first countries to develop a consumption tax based on value added. Following its introduction in a rudimentary form in 1965—when it was applied to the manufacture and importation of goods—the reforms of 1968, 1971, and 1974 focused on refining the tax concept, clarifying the credit principle, and rationalizing and augmenting the list of services included in the value-added tax (VAT) base. Nevertheless, changes such as those made in 1974 emphasized details and added complexity by widening the range of VAT rates, thus making the VAT more difficult to administer.

Further reforms of the tax structure that affected the VAT came in 1983–84, 1990–91, and 1992. The 1983–84 reforms extended the VAT to retail trade, streamlined the rate structure by consolidating many rates to a general rate of 10 percent, included more services in the base, and introduced improvements in administration by establishing procedures for exchanging information with the income tax office, as well as by simplifying the tax declaration procedure.

During the 1990–91 reforms, the general VAT rate was increased to 12 percent, and the services base was extended further. Some defects in the VAT structure continued: the range of rates (from 3 percent to 35 percent) was wide; credit for VAT paid on capital goods was excluded; there was a differential treatment in the calculation of credit; and important sectors, such as mining, electricity, water, and a high proportion of personal services, continued to be exempted from the VAT. However, the system was simplified by transferring a long list of zero-rated categories in agriculture to exempted status.[5]

The 1992 reforms increased the VAT rate to 14 percent for a period of five years starting in 1993 and widened the VAT base by including some services

previously exempted while exempting selected essential consumption goods and imported agricultural machinery. Rates of 35 percent and 45 percent were established for luxury items (such as jewelry and automobiles). A credit mechanism for VAT paid on purchases of capital goods was established in the form of a credit against income tax due.

With all the changes in structure, rate hikes, and administrative improvements, such as the development of a sophisticated tax declaration and payments system within the banking system, VAT revenues have increased. The VAT share of GDP rose from an average of approximately 2 percent in 1980–83 to approximately 3 percent in 1988–91 and nearly 5 percent in 1992–94. However, with general rates of 10 percent in 1990 and 12 percent in 1992, collections were still smaller in terms of GDP than, for example, in Chile.[6] The next two parts of this section elaborate on the particular factors that have determined Colombia's VAT performance.

Potential Versus Actual Revenue Collections

In light of the performance of the VAT in Colombia, the authorities became increasingly preoccupied with evasion of the VAT and its magnitude.[7] A study was consequently attempted that calculated potential VAT revenue using an available input-output matrix. The study then compared the result with the actual collection figure available from the tax administration.

Calculation Using Input-Output Matrix

Using the 1988 input-output matrix (the latest that was available), it was possible to conduct an exercise

---

Note: This section was prepared by Parthasarathi Shome.

[5]Under the zero rating of the VAT, there is full crediting of the VAT paid on purchases even while there is zero VAT on sales. Under the exemption rating, there is no credit when the product is not taxed. Typically, administering a zero-rated VAT structure for the agricultural sector is cumbersome.

[6]With a general VAT rate of 18 percent, Chile has exceeded 9 percent of GDP in VAT collection in recent years. This 50 percent "VAT productivity rate" is among the highest in the world.

[7]This is an issue that has concerned many country authorities. Based on initial technical assistance provided by the Fiscal Affairs Department of the IMF, some authorities now monitor VAT evasion on an annual basis. See Tanzi and Shome (1993).

on that year's potential VAT collections. The results of this exercise appear in Appendix II (see Table 20). Data on gross output and intermediate consumption in each sector were used. Bearing in mind that, prior to the passage of Law No. 49 in 1991, only a few parts of each sector were subject to the VAT and that differential rates were applied in various categories within each sector, the actual rates were calculated for each sector and its intermediate inputs. Gross payable VAT and the VAT creditable by sector were thus obtained. A similar process was used to determine the VAT assessable on imports and the VAT creditable against exports. The results of this exercise indicate that actual collections amounted to about two thirds of the potential.

Law No. 49 of 1991 expanded the potential VAT base further. The 1988 structure of the input-output matrix was thus again used to calculate the expanded base. The exercise, as shown in Table 21, Appendix II, introduced all the amendments represented by Law No. 49, effectively shifting agricultural products, fertilizers, and pharmaceuticals from zero-rated to exempted status, raising the general rate to 12 percent, and including some new personal services in the base.[8] Potential collections increased by almost 30 percent, with about one third of this increase pertaining to fertilizers and pharmaceuticals (including the effect of shifting these goods to the exempted category). Actual collections would then depend on the treatment in practice of these changes in the law.

A third exercise was carried out to examine potential VAT revenue on the assumption of an even greater hypothetical expansion of the VAT base than that brought about by Law No. 49. This exercise is presented in Table 22, Appendix II. The modifications introduced to the 1988 base in this case included (1) applying a general rate of 12 percent to all sectors, thus dismantling the differential rate structure;[9] (2) including all exempted products (such as mining, fertilizers, and pharmaceuticals) in the tax base, except for agricultural products; (3) giving credit for machinery and equipment, both domestic and imported; and (4) including in the tax base services that were still outside the base.[10] Treatment of the financial sector was left as in Law No. 49.[11]

The exercise indicated potential collections of over 10 percent above the potential amount yielded by the VAT structure reflecting Law No. 49 and of over 40 percent above the potential revenue from the structure in effect prior to Law No. 49. It bears noting that, according to this initial exercise, the cost of making all machinery and equipment eligible for credit would amount to less than 5 percent of potential collections.[12]

The effect of shifting mining from the exempted to the taxable list did not turn out to be significant, as a large portion of this sector's output is exported. The effect of broadening the base to include professional services was not insignificant, but in practice this increase would depend mainly on tax administration, as it would surely be very difficult to collect the full potential from this source. Revenue from beverages under these conditions would decrease, reflecting the application of the uniform—and lower—rate of 12 percent.[13] However, more revenue would be collected on newly taxed consumer items—for example, electricity, water, and construction.

The aim of considering this alternative was to examine the revenue impact of a VAT package that would further simplify its structure, broaden its base, and reduce the distortions that remained in the system after the introduction of Law No. 49. It can be concluded that these modifications would also result in a significant positive impact on potential revenue.

Calculations Made on the Basis of Declarations

As noted above, actual VAT revenue collected in 1988 was roughly two thirds of the potential (or theoretical) collections. What is the explanation for the revenue gap? The theoretical input-output matrix used in the calculations has a gross output base that

---

[8]Hotels with ratings of less than three stars, motels, charter flights, restaurants, video and electronic game rentals, bars, grills, discotheques, and cleaning establishments were included in the base.

[9]The administrative complications resulting from the differential rates, exemptions, and zero ratings, quite apart from the economic distortions that they cause, gave rise to more than 50 percent of the queries addressed to the legal division during the period September 1988–June 1991.

[10]Legal, accounting, technical, publicity, rental, security, medical, veterinary, theatrical and cultural services, as well as barbershops and beauty parlors, were included.

[11]Banks, life insurance, and other financial services were ex-

cluded because taxation of the financial sector is conceptually difficult. The problem with the financial sector, in general, is that while the other sectors pay interest, which forms part of the sector's value added, banks earn interest, resulting in negative value added. At the same time, life insurance has a sizable savings component that should not be targeted in a consumption tax. Some countries, such as Argentina, have experimented by levying the tax on proxy value added of this sector, derived by adding up its components to the most practicable extent.

[12]This is not surprising as most capital goods that were imported (and not produced in Colombia) were already exempted. Later, when Colombia made the remaining capital goods purchases creditable through Law No. 6 of 1992, a cross-check was conducted to determine the resulting loss in revenue. The result, which is dealt with below, is broadly consistent with the projections that have been made.

[13]It is obvious that if the VAT rate were made uniform, thereby bringing down the higher rates on luxury and scarce goods, there would be reason to introduce or increase the selective excises on goods in this category, including beverages, petroleum products, cigars, and automobiles. The rates would typically depend on revenue needs and conform to international standards.

Table 2. Comparison of Gross VAT and VAT Credited on the Basis of the Input-Output Matrix with VAT Calculated from Taxpayer Declarations, 1988
(In billions of Colombian pesos)

	Gross VAT (Net of Exports) (1)	VAT on Intermediate Consumption (2)	VAT on Imports (3)	Net VAT (4)
From input-output matrix (potential)[1]	567.2	200.0	154.1	521.3
From declarations (calculated)[2]	432.2	384.0	154.1[3]	202.3

Sources: Tax Studies Subdirectorate, Directorate of National Taxes; and IMF staff estimates.
[1]See Table 20.
[2]See Table 23.
[3]Assumption for purposes of the exercise.

is much larger than the base reflected in the VAT declarations of 1988, pointing to the impact of tax evasion and other leakages. Consequently, this section compares the calculations for collection made on the basis of information from VAT declarations (see Table 23, Appendix II) with the calculation of potential based on the input-output matrix.

Potential gross VAT, net of exports (see Tables 20 and 23, Appendix II), was derived from the 1988 input-output matrix in accordance with the prevailing VAT law. However, the actual declarations showed that taxpayers declared only 70 percent of gross income as subject to the VAT. Applying this correction factor, an amount of Col\$432.2 billion for calculated gross VAT was arrived at (Table 23, Appendix II).

The potential creditable VAT for intermediate consumption was also known from the previous exercise (Table 20, Appendix II). However, the declarations indicated that taxpayers declared 62 percent of gross VAT as creditable VAT. Using this correction factor, an amount of Col\$384 billion for VAT for calculated intermediate consumption was arrived at.

This exercise demonstrates that the taxable base calculated from the declarations was a great deal smaller than the theoretical base determined from the input-output matrix. For the exempted and zero-rated sectors, including exports, gross incomes were reduced in order to arrive at taxed incomes. As exports comprised less than one tenth of gross collections, the other exempted and zero-rated items had to account for the rest. The question then becomes, Why was the amount of zero ratings and exemptions in the declarations so much larger than the amounts implied by the matrix? This discrepancy reflects the gap between potential and actual collections.

Table 2 compares and contrasts the results from the exercises using the input-output matrix and the declarations. Column 2 of this table shows that the VAT credit from the declarations far exceed the theoretical credit according to the input-output matrix. This is yet another aspect of the gap between potential and calculated tax collections.

In conclusion, the figures for both gross VAT and VAT credit based on data obtained from the declarations differ significantly from those drawn directly from the input-output matrix, even when the VAT law is taken into account. The high level in the declarations of exemptions and zero ratings, and of credits claimed, points to the gap between potential and actual VAT collections.

Revenue Loss from Crediting VAT on Capital Goods

Law No. 6 of 1992 effectively transformed the VAT into a consumption-type VAT. Previously, the treatment had depended on the use of capital goods and on whether they were imported, thereby imparting a distortionary element to the VAT structure (Table 3). Nevertheless, most capital goods had been exempted; Law No. 6 simply extended full credit to capital goods that had not been exempted, although only against the income tax due. This change removed the earlier distortion, as the capital goods already exempted—the imported capital goods—had not caused distortions.[14] Also, the revenue cost of the

[14]Nevertheless, a few distortions remain. For example, see a peculiarity in Law No. 6 mentioned in footnote 3 of Table 3. Nevertheless, an examination of the tax data for 1993 revealed that, in its first year of operation, a large proportion of the VAT paid on capital goods was fully credited against the income tax.

Table 3. VAT Treatment of Capital Goods Before and After Passage of Law No. 6, 1992

Category[1]	Treatment Before Law No. 6	Treatment After Law No. 6
1. Not produced in Colombia and imported; used in a list of basic industries and in the petroleum sector.	Exempted from VAT.	Exempted from VAT.
2. Not produced in Colombia and imported; not used in basic industries.	VAT paid on purchase not creditable, although treated as cost in calculation of depreciation for income tax.[2]	VAT paid by companies creditable against their income tax.[3]
3. Produced in Colombia and imported.	As above.	As above.
4. Produced in Colombia and not imported.	As above.	As above.

Sources: National Directorate of Taxes and Customs; and IMF staff.[4]

[1]Capital goods used in the agricultural sector are exempted, mainly on administrative grounds.

[2]The revenue consequences of this treatment should be negligible, given the absence of inflation adjustment in that period despite an inflation rate of approximately 25 percent.

[3]There is a requirement that VAT credit on a capital good has to be returned by the taxpayer to the exchequer if it is sold before the termination of its useful life for tax purposes. Also, under Law No. 6, the credit is available for three years only, after which any excess credit has to be passed on as depreciable cost—which is the treatment that was in effect before Law No. 6.

[4]Prior to 1993, the Directorates of National Taxes and Customs were separate institutions. Information on the treatment of capital goods before the passage of Law No. 6 therefore comes from these two directorates.

change was expected to be low because of the relatively small proportion of capital goods involved.

The authorities were concerned, however, that the impact of the capital goods treatment in Law No. 6 on 1993 VAT revenue should be verified. This exercise was carried out by focusing on categories 2–4 of capital goods (Table 3), whose treatment was changed by Law No. 6, and by using sectoral information on the universe of large taxpayers in Bogotá, who accounted for 51 percent of the income tax collected in the country. The revenue loss for 1993 turned out to be approximately 0.2 percent of GDP, as derived from Table 24, Appendix II, a figure comparable to the revenue loss projected prior to the introduction of the law.[15]

Thus, the revenue loss, as anticipated, was small.

However, an additional question would be whether the loss would continue to be small in future years. The answer is difficult to formulate because nontax factors are often more important than tax factors in determining investment. Nevertheless, the information from Table 24, Appendix II can be utilized to obtain some indications. For example, VAT credit for capital goods increased threefold between 1992 and 1993 in nominal terms. Given the inflation rate of 25 percent and recalling that Law No. 6 became effective in the second half of 1992, it may be inferred that investment in categories 2–4 of capital goods (Table 3) increased by 10 percent in real terms between 1992 and 1993. That was a substantially higher rate than the rates of economic growth for the two years, 3.5 percent and 5 percent, respectively. Probably, therefore, the major part of the increase in investment in response to the change in the VAT treatment of capital goods resulting from Law No. 6 has already taken place. This conclusion implies only a small increase in revenue loss in future years.

---

[15]See the row for "machinery and equipment" in Table 22, Appendix II, for the calculation of revenue loss from making the VAT paid on machinery and equipment completely creditable, that is, a consumption-type VAT.

III Income Tax Issues

Three preoccupations have loomed large in the minds of the Colombian authorities with respect to income taxes: (1) the effect of income taxes on investment; (2) as in the case of the value-added tax (VAT), the magnitude of the tax evasion; and (3) the revenue impact of the recently introduced inflation adjustment and the further modifications that might be needed in it. The analyses carried out in these areas are presented in this section.

Tax Reform and Investment

A major concern of the Colombian authorities has been the secular decline in economic growth through much of the 1970s and 1980s (see Ocampo (1991) and (1992)), which culminated in a low of 2.1 percent in 1991. Understandably, the authorities became concerned about the investment climate. Although the fall in the long-term growth rate may not necessarily be attributable to a fall in capital accumulation—the investment rate at constant prices has been fairly stable in the past two decades—it was generally believed that the Colombian tax system introduced a bias against investment. If this bias was removed, capital accumulation would accelerate, as would growth.

Reform has thus been focused on making the income tax more neutral to investment and its composition. Replacement of the corporation income tax by a cash-flow tax, which is conceptually a tax on consumption, has been sometimes suggested in the literature as a way of attaining this objective, as it discounts investment immediately. However, this tax has not yet been applied in any country.[16] Several

forms of taxation of presumptive income, instead of actual income, have also been advocated.[17] The preferred form is a flat-rate tax on the companies' gross assets, on the grounds that such a tax would encourage investment in companies that are able to extract from their assets a higher-than-average return and penalize the ones that get only a lower-than-average return.[18] Such proposals have not been implemented in Colombia, although a concern about the effects of income taxation upon the incentives to invest was present in all the income tax reforms of the past decade.

In recent years, Colombia experienced three important direct tax reforms—in 1986, 1990, and 1992. These reforms were designed to prevent double taxation of enterprises and individuals and to remove obstacles to investment from the Colombian tax system. The 1986 reform gradually unified the profit tax rates of corporations and limited companies at 30 percent, which was identical to the highest marginal rate of individual income and capital gains taxes, while eliminating the tax on capital gains for stock transactions conducted through the stock exchange. After payment of the 30 percent company tax, the dividends paid out of the remaining 70 percent of the profits were exempted from the individual income tax. Hence, the reforms reduced the gap between the marginal productivity of capital and the rate of return obtained by individuals. Also, beginning in 1991, the capital gains tax was eliminated.

The 1992 reform introduced a method for the overall adjustment of taxes for inflation. It also extended the tax base to include state-owned enterprises, eliminated an additional tax on enterprises based on net worth, imposed a special five-year contribution on high-income persons (both natural and juridical), reduced the foreign remittance tax, and exempted foreign investment funds from taxation. A summary of

Note: In this section, "Tax Reform and Investment" was prepared by Erik Haindl; "Potential Versus Actual Revenue Collections" by David Dunn; and "Inflation Adjustment" by Osvaldo Schenone.

[16]See, for instance, Shome and Schutte (1993), and the references quoted therein. They conclude that the cash-flow tax "remains a theoretically attractive option with some practical disadvantages. Moreover, many unanswered questions remain for its implementation by a single country—especially a developing one—in an environment that will not necessarily accommodate its smooth and effective operation."

[17]For an early treatment of this issue, see Tanzi (1991).

[18]On this subject, see Sadka and Tanzi (1993). These authors traced back the idea to a seventeenth-century tax in the Principality of Milan, as reported by Carlo Cattaneo in 1839, who was quoted in turn by Einaudi (1959).

Table 4. Summary of Direct Tax Rates
(In percent)

	1986	1989	1992
Corporate taxes			
Net income of corporations	40	30	30
Net income of limited liabilities	18	30	30
Capital gains	40 or 18	30	30
Minimum income tax	8 percent net assets or 2 percent net revenue	8 percent net assets or 2 percent net revenue	7 percent net assets
Branch profits remitted abroad	20	20	19
Other payments remitted abroad	12	12	12
Foreign income	Taxed	Taxed	Taxed
Stock dividends	Taxed	Not taxed	Not taxed
Intercompany dividends	64 percent of dividends are taxed	Not taxed	Not taxed
Individual taxes			
Total income	0–49	0–30	0–30
Interest income	0–49	0–30	0–30
Dividend income	0–49	Not taxed	Not taxed
Capital gains on stocks	10–24.5	0–30	Not taxed
Other capital gains	10–24.5	0–30	0–30

Source: Price Waterhouse.

the main changes introduced by these reforms in direct taxes is indicated in Table 4.

There have been some further reform proposals, including McLure's (1988), which supported implementation of a consumption-type cash-flow tax to induce a higher level of savings and investment. However, the main practical drawback to this tax is that the United States and other capital exporting countries might not allow a foreign tax credit for a consumption-based tax. Therefore, the reforms have proceeded along traditional lines, incorporating nevertheless the express objective of accelerating economic growth.

However, the tax system was not the only element to play a role in the investment decisions in the Colombian economy. Other elements included a foreign exchange shortage, particularly in connection with the Latin American debt crisis in 1982; a domestic financing constraint, induced by the authorities' anti-inflationary policy; and structural trends associated with the "Dutch disease" effect of the coffee boom of the 1970s and the easy access to external financing.[19]

Nevertheless, the authorities are eager to reach a clearer understanding of the impact of the 1986 tax reform on investment. The objective of the following exercise is therefore to explore quantitatively the potential impact of the 1986 tax reform on the investment rate. It is found that the tax reform of 1986 had a positive impact on investment. However, this positive impact was offset by other structural factors that took place simultaneously.

Assessing the User Cost of Capital

Appendix III describes the methodology used to estimate the user cost of capital and the marginal consumption sacrifice. The main difficulty encountered in estimating these values related to the updating of the capital stock series for Colombia.[20] It was therefore decided to build a capital stock series, based on a "one-hoss-shay"—or onetime—depreciation, which was then used to compute the user cost of capital presented in Appendix III. The resulting user cost of capital series for Colombia shows a declining trend, which reached 15.2 percent in 1991 (Table 5).

The user cost of capital can be interpreted in various ways, which are equivalent in equilibrium. First, the user cost of capital can be interpreted as the

[19]See Ocampo (1991) and Edwards (1984).

[20]More dated capital stock series for Colombia were available. See, for example, Harberger (1969) and Clavijo (1990), among others.

Table 5. User Cost of Capital
(In percent per year; in real terms)

Period	Rate
Average 1970–79	19.8
Average 1980–85	17.9
1986	16.8
1987	16.6
1988	16.1
1989	15.6
1990[1]	15.3
1991[1]	15.2

Source: IMF staff estimates.

[1]Values for 1990 and 1991 have been estimated by taking into account the real interest rates of the financial system and the risk premium for 1989.

Table 6. Gap in the Savings-Investment Market
(In percent)

Year	Marginal Productivity of Capital	Marginal Consumption Sacrifice	Savings-Investment Gap
1986	16.8	6.1	10.7
1987	16.6	9.9	6.7
1988	16.1	9.4	6.7
1989	15.6	9.3	6.3

Source: IMF staff estimates.

"rent" that an enterprise pays to lease a unit of physical capital. This rent depends on the price of the capital good, the interest rate, the taxes on earnings of capital, and economic depreciation.

A second way to visualize the user cost of capital acknowledges the fact that the large majority of enterprises buys capital goods using a combination of their own resources (equity capital) and borrowed resources (debt). The capital user cost is the minimum return that the purchased capital must yield in order to be able to pay the taxes, plus the minimum returns demanded by shareholders (equity capital) and creditors (debt). That is, the user cost of capital is the discount rate applied to the profile of the expected returns on a project to determine whether it is beneficial for an enterprise.

A third way to look at the user cost of capital is to recognize that, in maximizing their profits, enterprises will increase their capital until its marginal productivity is equal to the cost of using the capital. In this sense, the user cost of capital represents the marginal productivity of capital in equilibrium.

As indicated in Appendix III, the methodology used to measure the cost of using capital in Colombia is Harberger's (1969). To measure the marginal consumption sacrifice and to quantify the gap on the savings-investment market (that is, the difference between the marginal productivity of capital and the marginal consumption sacrifice), the economic agents in that market are assumed to be subject to marginal individual tax rates in the highest bracket.

Savings-Investment Gap

Direct taxes introduce a wedge between the interest and dividend payments by enterprises and what the owners of capital effectively receive. This wedge constitutes the difference between the marginal productivity of capital and the marginal consumption sacrifice. As shown in Table 6, the savings-investment gap was reduced by about 4.4 percentage points (almost one half) as a result of the 1986 tax reform.[21]

The market risk premium is equivalent to the difference between the rate of return required by individuals on a market portfolio and a risk-free obligation. Estimated as a by-product of the methodology developed in Appendix III, the premium was about 12 percent in 1989 (Table 7). This premium is lower than that estimated by Carrizosa (1986) for an earlier period (15 percent), but it is high by international standards.

Effect of 1986 Tax Reform on the Investment Rate

The effect of the reduction in the savings-investment gap on the investment rate depends critically on the interest elasticity of the savings and investment schedules. The higher the absolute magnitudes of the elasticities of both schedules, the greater will be the impact of the tax reform on equilibrium investment.

In order to assess the quantitative impacts of the tax reform, a disaggregated simultaneous equation model for savings and private investment was developed. This is presented in Appendix IV. Private savings depend on variables such as the tax burden,

---

[21]The tax reform passed in late 1990 should have reduced it even further as a direct consequence of the elimination of the capital gains tax on shares of stock and the application of the inflation adjustment, which took effect in 1991 and 1992, respectively. This new reduction in the gap should have had a positive impact on the investment rate. In 1991, at the time of conducting this study, it was too early to assess the impact of the reduction.

Table 7. Market Risk Premium
(In percent)

Year	Rate of Return on Shares (After taxes)	Rate of Return on Debt (After taxes)	Market Risk Premium
1986	13.0	3.9	9.1
1987	19.3	3.8	15.5
1988	18.4	2.9	15.5
1989	16.3	4.2	12.1

Source: IMF staff estimates.

Chart 1. Investment and Savings
(In percent)

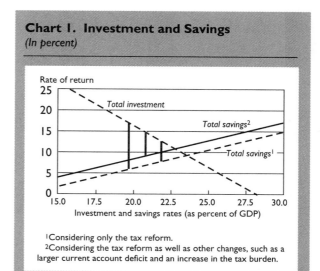

[1]Considering only the tax reform.
[2]Considering the tax reform as well as other changes, such as a larger current account deficit and an increase in the tax burden.

public savings, external savings, and the rate of return on savings (or marginal consumption sacrifice), and private investment is assumed to depend on the user cost of capital. Simple dynamic effects are allowed. Public savings, external savings, and public investment are considered exogenous variables in the model.

There are two main conclusions from the model. First, the 1986 tax reform had a positive impact on the investment rate. The reform caused marginal tax rates for individuals to go down and eliminated the double taxation of individuals and enterprises, thereby reducing the gap between the user cost of capital and the marginal consumption sacrifice. As a result, investment rose by 1.2 percent of GDP, induced in its entirety by increased private savings and private investment. Second, this potential positive impact was partially neutralized by structural factors, such as a decrease in external savings and an increase in the direct tax burden.

Table 8 presents data evaluating the various fac-

tors that came into play during the period 1983–89. In 1989, the total investment rate was 0.6 percent of GDP higher than in 1983. While the 1986 tax reform lowered marginal tax rates and, owing to the reduction in the savings-investment gap, increased the investment rate by 1.2 percent of GDP, total tax revenues rose because of a bigger effort to reduce tax evasion. Direct tax revenues increased by 1.4 percent of GDP during 1983–89. Indirect tax revenues were 2.3 percent of GDP higher in 1989 than in 1983. This increased tax burden implied a negative income effect for the private sector, which experienced reduced private savings, and, hence, a reduction in the investment rate of 0.7 percent of GDP. There was also an increase in public savings of 5.1 percent of GDP between 1983 and 1989, which had a positive impact of 1.6 percent of GDP on total investment.[22] Another important factor had a negative influence on total investment: the decrease in external savings (reflected, in turn, as a decrease in the current account deficit of the balance of payments), which reached 6.7 percent of GDP.[23] This reduction in external savings caused a fall in total investment by some 2 percent of GDP. All these effects are illustrated in Chart 1. Finally, there is an unexplained residual that accounts for a positive increase in investment of 0.5 percent of GDP.

Table 8. Increase in Investment Rates, 1983–89
(In percent of GDP)

	Change in Variable	Effect on Investment
Increase in indirect tax burden	2.3	—
Increase in direct tax burden	1.4	−0.7
Increase in public savings	5.1	1.6
Decrease in external savings	6.7	−2.0
Tax reform	—	1.2
Residual (other factors)	—	0.5
Total change in investment rate between 1983 and 1989	—	0.6

Source: IMF staff estimates.

[22]In fact, public savings increased by more than the change in total tax revenues, which is consistent with the contractionary fiscal policy followed during that period by the Colombian authorities.

[23]This decrease in the current account deficit represents a reduction of capital inflows, perhaps reflecting to some extent the impact of the Latin American debt crisis and the high real exchange rate policy pursued during this period (see Tanzi and Chu (1992)).

Table 9. Impact on the Investment Rate
(In percent of GDP)

1 Percent of GDP Change in the Variable	Effect on Total Investment (Short-term)	Effect on Total Investment (Long-term)	Effect on Private Savings (Long-term)	Effect on Private Investment (Long-term)
Increase in direct taxes (keeping public savings constant)	−0.43	−0.50	−0.50	−0.50
Increase in direct taxes (increasing public savings with these resources)	−0.15	−0.18	−1.18	−0.18
Increase in direct taxes (increasing public investment with these resources)	0.21	0.08	−0.92	−0.92
Reduction in public savings	−0.28	−0.32	0.68	−0.32
Reduction in external savings	−0.26	−0.30	0.70	−0.30

Source: IMF staff estimates.

Specific Impacts on the Investment Rate

The long-term effects during the period 1970–85 indicate that, for every increase in the direct tax burden of 1 percent of GDP, the rate of investment in the Colombian economy fell by about 0.5 percent of GDP. Moreover, a decrease in external savings equivalent to 1 percent of GDP caused a drop in investment of approximately 0.30 percent of GDP. Similarly, an increase in public savings equivalent to 1 percent of GDP led to an increase in the investment rate estimated at 0.32 percent of GDP. A summary of the estimated impact of the factors that affected the investment rate is shown in Table 9, taking into account just the income effect of an increased tax burden.[24]

Table 9 indicates that an increase in direct taxation for government consumption purposes would have the biggest negative influence on investment. A rise in direct taxes to finance government consumption of 1 percent of GDP, if accomplished by increasing marginal tax rates, would cause a decline of 0.88 percent of GDP in total investment in the long run (0.50 percent owing to an increased tax burden and 0.38 percent to a widening in the savings-investment gap). If the same increase were accomplished by reducing tax evasion, only the income effect would be

present, and total investment would be reduced by 0.50 percent of GDP.

No significant effect of the indirect tax burden on investment was found. This means that private consumption experienced most of the income effect associated with an increased indirect tax burden in Colombia. Therefore, a rise in indirect taxes to finance government consumption of 1 percent of GDP could cause no measurable effect on total investment. Only a substitution of private consumption for public consumption should have taken place.

An increase in direct taxes of 1 percent of GDP to finance public investment, if accomplished by changing marginal tax rates, should have a negative long run impact of 0.30 percent of GDP in total investment. This would be the combined result of three effects: an income effect generated by the increased direct tax burden, which reduces investment by 0.50 percent of GDP; a substitution effect caused by a widening savings-investment gap, which would reduce investment by a further 0.38 percent of GDP; and a direct effect arising from increased public investment, which would have a positive impact on total investment of 0.58 percent of GDP. The latter effect is not a complete replacement (where a 1 percent rise in public investment increases total investment by 1 percent) because some crowding out of private investment would take place, owing to a higher interest rate (see Appendix IV). However, an increase in indirect taxes of 1 percent of GDP to finance public investment would have a positive impact of 0.58 percent of GDP on total investment. The results of the econometric model suggest that only the direct effect would take place.

Other interesting results are related to the effect of

---

[24]An increase in direct taxation would normally be associated with higher marginal tax rates, which produce both income and substitution effects. If this were the case, increased rates that collected 1 percent more of GDP would imply a widening of the savings-investment gap, which would reduce the investment rate by a further 0.33 percent of GDP in the short run and 0.38 percent of GDP in the long run. This outcome can be derived from the S = I estimated equation in Appendix IV.

public savings. An increase in public savings of 1 percent of GDP, if accomplished by reducing government consumption, would have a positive impact on total investment of 0.32 percent of GDP. The impact would not be one-to-one because of some crowding-out effects on private savings (see Appendix IV).

If the increase in public savings achieved by reducing government consumption were used to finance public investment, there would be a positive impact on total investment of 1 percent of GDP. In other words, switching from government consumption to public investment would have a one-to-one effect on total investment. In other cases, where the private sector is affected by income or substitution effects, some crowding out would occur.

If an increase in public sector savings of 1 percent of GDP were achieved by raising direct taxes through the use of higher marginal tax rates, there would be a decline in total investment of 0.56 percent of GDP. This would be the combined result of a fall in investment (owing to an income effect of 0.50 percent of GDP); a further decline in investment by 0.38 percent of GDP (caused by a widening of the savings-investment gap); and a positive impact on investment of 0.32 percent of GDP (owing to the increased public sector savings).

If an increase in public sector savings of 1 percent of GDP were achieved by raising indirect taxes, there would be an increase in total investment of 0.32 percent of GDP.

The change in external savings—the deficit of the current account of the balance of payments—also has a significant impact on total investment. An increase in external savings of 1 percent of GDP would increase total investment by 0.30 percent of GDP. The impact is not one-to-one because of an induced reduction in private savings generated by a crowding-out effect.

In Colombia, this change in external savings has been the single most important factor inducing a decline in total investment rates. As mentioned above, external savings were reduced by 6.7 percent of GDP between 1983 and 1989, which reduced the total investment rate by some 2 percent of GDP. The policy of high real exchange rates pursued by the Colombian Government, together with the implementation of restrictive fiscal and monetary policies, caused a significant improvement in the current account. In fact, the 1983 current account deficit of 5.2 percent of GDP was transformed into a current account surplus of 1.5 percent of GDP by 1989. However, this important macroeconomic result also reduced external savings and negatively affected the investment rate.

To conclude, had the 1986 tax reform not taken place, there would have been a decline in the total

investment rate from 1983 to 1989. The tax reform, together with other positive factors, such as the increase in public savings, prevented this situation from materializing.

Potential Versus Actual Revenue Collections

As in the case of the VAT, the authorities have been concerned with the extent of the evasion of income taxes. A study was therefore undertaken with the objective of quantifying income tax evasion, using as a basis initial endeavors by the Directorate of National Taxes (DIN).

A Summary of Studies Initiated by the DIN

The Center for Fiscal Studies (CEF) of the DIN initiated studies in 1992–93 that provided a good first approximation of income tax evasion over the period 1987–91. The studies used the "revenue gap" approach, which measures the difference between actual tax collections and potential revenue, as calculated by applying the tax law to relevant economic indicators. In addition to yielding credible estimates of overall income tax evasion, the CEF studies made use of data on tax collections by sector and type of taxpayer (namely, corporations and individuals) to produce disaggregated estimates of evasion (Table 10).

The key element in the CEF procedure is the use of the gross operating surplus (EBE)[25] in the national accounts as the measure of potential business income net of labor costs and purchases of materials or intermediate goods (see Table 11). To yield a figure that is more closely related to the concept of taxable income (RA), the studies subtracted from EBE estimates of income not subject to the income tax (IF), deductible interest payments (CD), and allowances for depreciation, amortization, and depletion (CF). The tax law further specifies income that is exempt from the income tax (RD), so one more adjustment was necessary before potential taxable income (RE_p) was obtained. Applying an effective tax rate to this figure and subtracting other creditable taxes yielded the final figure for potential tax revenue. Tax evasion was then calculated as the difference between potential revenue and actual tax collections, divided by potential revenue.

Because of the different tax treatment of corporations and self-employed individuals, the CEF studies derived evasion estimates for each group of tax-

---

[25]The acronyms used are the Spanish ones in order to facilitate comparability for the researcher interested in dealing with Colombian sources.

Table 10. Estimates of Income Tax Evasion by the Center for Fiscal Studies
(In percent)

	1987	1988	1989	1990	1991
In percent of potential revenue					
Overall	33.2	38.1	32.2	28.5	28.6
Corporations	30.0	34.3	29.0	24.2	24.2
Agriculture	87	83	87	82	82
Mining	20	19	8	8	5
Manufacturing	12	11	10	10	6
Construction	46	61	65	75	62
Commerce, restaurants, and hotels	45	51	42	41	45
Transportation, storage, and communication	75	86	73	54	51
Finance	19	17	10	8	5
Services	8	18	48	35	37
Individuals	46.9	53.8	47.1	57.1	57.6
Agriculture	33	35	24	69	61
Mining	52	62	51	31	33
Manufacturing	76	72	67	69	65
Construction	58	70	72	75	74
Commerce, restaurants, and hotels	56	72	60	65	80
Transportation, storage, and communication	73	83	84	85	75
Finance	16	30	37	23	25
Services	41	53	57	54	75
In percent of GDP					
Overall	1.15	1.55	1.31	1.12	1.08
Corporations	0.84	1.13	0.97	0.83	0.79
Individuals	0.31	0.42	0.34	0.29	0.28

Source: The Center for Fiscal Studies, Directorate of National Taxes.

payers separately.[26] Also, in applying this procedure, the CEF studies relied heavily on information from actual tax returns. In fact, *EBE* was the only economic indicator used in the study that was not derived from tax returns. The distribution of *EBE* to the different categories of taxpayers and the determination of the components in calculating potential tax revenue were based on ratios of corresponding items in the tax declarations. For example, to divide *EBE* between corporations and individuals, the CEF studies used the share of gross income for each group as reported in the tax return data. Similarly, the deductions, such as depreciation allowances, were estimated by multiplying the share of *EBE* apportioned to the category under study by the share of the particular deduction in the gross income concept derived from the tax returns.[27] Use of this procedure

shows that evasion is essentially determined by the initial allocation of *EBE* to the group under study.

The remaining elements of the potential tax revenue calculation were derived in a similar manner from tax return data. Exempted taxable income was based on the ratio of *RD* to *RA* in the tax declarations, the effective tax rate was determined by the ratio of tax liability (*LA*) to net taxable income (*RE*), and the potential tax credit was the ratio of the credit (*LB*) to *LA* times the potential tax liability. Such calculations again suggest that the relative measure of evasion depends on the initial ratio of *EBE* to the gross income derived from the tax returns.

An Alternative Approach

The CEF approach had to be refined so that the components of the potential tax revenue calculation

---

[26]As mentioned above, while corporations are taxed at a flat 30 percent rate, self-employed individuals are taxed according to a progressive tax schedule, with a maximum rate of 30 percent applicable.

[27]As explained in Table 11, *EBE* corresponds in the studies to income net of operating costs before exemptions (*RA*), plus de-

preciation, amortization, and depletion allowances (*CF*), plus interest deductions (*CD*), plus revenues not constituting income or profits (*IF*). Depreciation allowances for group *i* would then be equal to

$$EBE_i \times CF/(RA + CF + CD + IF).$$

Table 11. Formula Used by the Center for Fiscal Studies to Estimate Income Tax Evasion

Declaration of Income	Code	National Accounts
Income		
Net sales	IA	Gross operating surplus (EBE)
Services, honoraria, and commissions	IB	
Interest and financial earnings	IC	
Dividends	ID	
Other income	IE	
(−) Less revenues not constituting income or profits	IF	$IF/(RA + IF + CD + CF)\ EBE = IFp$ (potential)
Total income (IA through IF)	IG	
Costs		
Initial inventory	CA	
Purchases of materials	CB	
Wages and salaries	CC	
Interest and other financial expenses	CD	$CD/(RA + IF + CD + CF)\ EBE = CDp$ (potential)
Commissions, honoraria, and services	CE	
Depreciation and depletion allowances	CF	$CF/(RA + IF + CD + CF)\ EBE = CFp$ (potential)
Other costs and deductions	CG	
(−) Less final inventory	CH	
Total costs and deductions (CA through CH)	CI	
Net income (IG − CI)	RA	$EBE - IF - CD - CF = RAp$ (potential)
(−) Less nontaxable income	RD	$(RD/RA)\ RAp = RDp$
Taxable income (RA − RD)	RE	$RAp - RDp = REp$
Tax on taxable income (RE * Tax Rate)	LA	$REp\ (LA/RE) = LAp$
(−) Less tax credits	LB	$(LB/LA)\ LAp = LBp$
Net income tax (LA − LB)	LC	$LAp - LBp = LCp$

Source: Special Administrative Unit, Directorate of National Taxes.

could be independently verified. A more thorough analysis, estimating specific elements of the potential revenue independently, was needed not only to improve the accuracy of the evasion estimates, but also to provide greater insight into the problem areas of tax administration. In response to these concerns, therefore, this analysis was attempted.

In a sense, this alternative approach is analogous to an aggregated tax audit. Just as a tax auditor looks for independent line-by-line verification when reviewing an individual taxpayer's return, this approach searches for data to verify each line in the aggregated tax declarations. While the approach clearly requires a more intensive data search—as applied to 1987–91 tax collections—it offers the potential benefit of identifying specific areas in which taxpayers may overreport deductions or underreport income.

As noted above, EBE, which is a measure of the gross return to capital, is an appropriate measure of income net of labor and material costs. However, typical national accounting conventions suggest that EBE will contain some items that are not appropriate for the income tax base and will exclude other items that are. In particular, national accounting often includes under EBE estimates for the implicit rental income of owner-occupied housing, the informal sector of the economy, and income from illegal activities. However, EBE does not take into account interest and dividend earnings, which, although essentially mechanisms for distributing EBE to the owners of capital, are included in taxable income.[28]

Appendix V provides the details regarding the adjustment made to EBE. Table 35, Appendix V divides EBE between corporations and individuals and, after introducing appropriate adjustments relating to imputed income from owner-occupied housing, illegal activities, interest, and inflation adjustment, obtains the adjusted income for tax purposes. Table 36, Appendix V, calculates separately for corporations and individuals the depreciation allowances for various categories of capital goods.

It is therefore possible to calculate roughly potential tax revenue (see Table 12), as the estimated components of taxable income can be used to derive potential taxable income. Specially exempted income has been excluded from this calculation, but a brief investigation of the relative importance of co-

---

[28]Dividends earned by firms that hold shares of other firms are generally not taxable, if tax was paid on the income of the subsidiary firm.

Table 12. Calculation of Potential Taxable Income and Income Tax Evasion
(In millions of current Colombian pesos, unless otherwise specified)

	1987	1988	1989	1990	1991	1992
Corporations						
(1) Adjusted income for taxes	2,562,514	3,405,550	4,700,835	6,394,689	8,188,369	9,886,385
(2) Interest deduction	983,876	1,228,691	1,755,622	2,235,968	2,722,161	2,537,076
(3) Depreciation, amortization, and depletion allowances	507,713	709,293	980,202	1,295,607	1,662,628	1,910,615
(4) Taxable income = (1) − (2) − (3)	1,070,925	1,467,565	1,965,011	2,863,113	3,803,580	5,438,694
(5) Potential tax revenue	321,278	440,270	589,503	858,934	1,141,074	1,641,493
(6) Exemptions, credits, and losses adjustment (in percent)	6.9	5.3	7.2	7.9	8.7	7.25
(7) Potential tax revenue = (5) − [(4) × (6)]	247,583	362,411	447,971	632,085	810,139	1,247,183
(8) Actual tax declared	173,392	254,319	358,871	524,562	655,526	...
(9) Relative evasion (in percent) = [(7) − (8)]/(7)	30.0	29.8	19.9	17.0	19.1	...
Individuals						
(10) Adjusted income for taxes	1,570,593	2,055,832	2,614,503	3,552,430	4,633,796	6,046,229
(11) Interest deduction	229,375	342,994	513,462	667,500	870,688	1,136,084
(12) Depreciation, amortization, and depletion allowances	56,735	90,674	129,292	169,669	223,844	253,971
(13) Taxable income = (10) − (11) − (12)	1,284,483	1,622,164	1,971,749	2,715,261	3,539,263	4,656,174
(14) Effective tax rate (in percent)	4.1	4.2	4.2	5.2	6.2	4.8
(15) Potential tax revenue = (13) × (14)	52,729	68,394	83,586	141,558	218,059	223,496
(16) Actual tax declared	32,796	42,821	55,641	75,930	106,904	...
(17) Relative evasion (in percent) = [(15) − (16)]/(15)	37.8	37.4	33.4	46.4	51.0	...
Total						
(18) Potential tax revenue = (7) + (15)	300,312	430,805	531,557	773,643	1,028,198	1,470,679
(19) Actual tax declared = (8) + (16)	206,188	297,140	414,512	600,492	762,430	...
(20) Overall relative evasion (in percent) = [(18) − (19)]/(18)	31.2	30.9	21.9	22.4	25.8	...

Source: IMF staff estimates.

operatives and community enterprises would allow a rough estimate to be made of this element. The estimate for potential tax revenue is then calculated by applying the statutory tax rate of 30 percent for corporations and the effective tax rate—derived from the data from tax declarations—for individuals.[29]

The above-described procedure indicates that tax evasion among individuals has been particularly severe, increasing from about 38 percent in 1987 to 51 percent in 1991. However, corporate income tax evasion fell from 30 percent to 19 percent during the same time period. Given the weight of the latter, overall income tax evasion fell from 31 percent to 26 percent (Table 12).

The results largely reflect the shifting of interest deductions and depreciation allowances to corporations and the attribution by the national accounts of a majority of *EBE* to individuals, in sharp contrast to the implications of the data from the tax declarations. The exercise is, on the whole, a preliminary attempt at measuring income tax evasion: it was one of the first attempted using a set of Latin American data,

and it could be improved upon in the future.[30] For example, the data from the tax returns indicate substantial figures for "other income" and "other deductions." Clearly, what these categories stand for should be investigated, and an attempt should be made to use independent sources to measure them.

Improving the Procedures

Three basic procedures could be utilized to maximize the results of the administrative efforts. First, as indicated above, a deeper search could be made for independent sources of data to verify various components of the calculated potential tax base. Just as an actual income tax audit would seek to verify a firm's revenue and expenses, it would be useful to verify the tax returns at an aggregated level. Much of the necessary data for this analysis does exist, but it is a matter of sorting them for analytical purposes. The data might reveal substantial differences between the components of potential taxable income and the ac-

---

[29]If more time had been available, a final adjustment for credits could have been made by using more detailed data from the tax declarations.

[30]A first attempt was made in a similar vein by Aguirre and Shome (1988) to measure VAT evasion in Mexico. Subsequently, as mentioned in Section II, the methodology was further streamlined and applied to many other Latin American countries.

tual declarations. Detailed procedures for estimating income tax evasion are not yet common, and, in continuing this initial exercise, further refinements might be attempted.

Second, as Herschel (1975) points out, information from surveys and audits could provide valuable information on the breakdown of evasion between underreporting and nonreporting. Studies complemented with auditing results should reveal areas of strength and weakness in tax administration and aid the authorities in better directing their administrative resources and designing easier-to-enforce tax policies.

Third, a more thorough disaggregated analysis of tax evasion at the sectoral level might be undertaken. For example, if a major source of tax revenue, such as the oil industry, is well monitored and thought to have only minor evasion problems, it could be excluded from the sample so that evasion can be more precisely identified elsewhere in the economy.[31] Such useful disaggregated data should be available from the national accounts.

Inflation Adjustment

The annual rate of inflation in Colombia during the 1990s has varied between 22 percent and 30 percent. The presence of inflation creates gains and losses that will be overlooked by ordinary accounting procedures and, hence, ignored in the determination of taxable income. Inflation adjustment was adopted in Colombia in 1992 to solve this problem. While the procedure adopted is essentially correct, it should be emphasized that the authorities' focus has been on identifying the corrections needed to maximize revenues under this procedure.

The Nature of the Problem

Inflation adjustment is not intended to eliminate inflation-created gains and losses, but to include them in the tax base with all other gains and losses. To identify such gains and losses, it is convenient to consider separately monetary and nonmonetary assets and liabilities in the balance sheet of firms. Monetary assets and liabilities are those whose values are eroded by inflation, such as cash in the vault or accounts payable (or receivable) in local currency. However, the value of nonmonetary assets or liabilities, such as buildings, inventories, or accounts payable (or receivable) in foreign currency or in kind, is protected from inflation. Only monetary assets can experience inflation-created losses,

and only monetary liabilities can experience inflation-created gains, as illustrated by the following example.

Suppose that a company buys a piece of machinery with a loan made in Colombian pesos. The accounts will show identical increases in total assets and liabilities. Moreover, under an annual inflation rate of 20 percent, the balance sheet will show no change after one year. The reality, however, is very different. With the mere passing of time, the value of the debt (assuming, for simplicity, that no amortization takes place during the year) has been eroded by one fifth, although the machinery is still intact. This constitutes a gain, which inflation adjustment would make taxable.

Another way of looking at the situation is to realize that, without inflation adjustment, the firm would deduct as a cost interest on the loan (for example, 25 percent per year if the real rate of interest is 5 percent), ignoring the fact that four fifths of that deduction really represents the inflationary erosion of the debt rather than a true cost. Such an omission is precisely what the inflation adjustment aims to correct.

In this example, the gain takes place in the monetary liability, not in the nonmonetary asset. In fact, the inflation-created gain would not have existed if the asset had been bought using own capital instead of debt, or if the firm had been required to repay the debt by delivering 100 tons of merchandise or US$100,000.[32]

Thus, the inflation adjustment of taxable profits consists of adding to the standard (unadjusted) profits the following:

(Monetary Liabilities − Monetary Assets) × Inflation Rate.

This way of expressing the inflation adjustment, however, encounters strong resistance from accountants on two grounds. First, if monetary liabilities are adjusted, their value will no longer equal the amount of nominal debt originally contracted. Hence, when the debt is repaid, the account will fail to show a zero balance.

Second, if monetary assets are adjusted, several difficulties arise. First, the adjusted value of cash in the vault will not be equal to the amount of cash actually in the vault. Although, from an accounting viewpoint, Col$1,000 in January and Col$1,000 in December should be the same, inflation makes their values very different from one another in reality. Second, the value of accounts receivable will no

---

[31]The disaggregated data could be usefully consolidated for the purpose of carrying out more detailed analyses of tax evasion.

[32]Regardless of the existence of inflation, 100 tons of merchandise or US$100,000 will still have the same real value, although the nominal value may be very different. That is, inflation-created gains or losses cannot exist unless a monetary asset or liability is involved.

longer be equal to the original value. Hence, when the debtor repays his debt to the company, the accounts receivable item will fail to show a zero balance.

Although these objections may be of no consequence from an economic viewpoint, they create problems for accountants. Therefore, an equivalent procedure may be devised to overcome these accountancy objections. Given the identity

Monetary Assets + Nonmonetary Assets = Monetary Liabilities + Nonmonetary Liabilities + Net Worth,

then

Monetary Liabilities − Monetary Assets = Nonmonetary Assets − Nonmonetary Liabilities − Net Worth.

Therefore, inflation-created profits and losses of any particular year can be alternatively written as

(Nonmonetary Assets − Nonmonetary Liabilities − Net Worth) × Inflation Rate.

This is the way in which company profits are adjusted by inflation in Colombia, with certain variations.

Inflation Adjustment in Colombia

Inventories are adjusted by using a quarterly average of the annual rate of inflation for the purchases in each quarter. However, given that monthly rates of inflation are readily available, it would be more accurate to use the actual rates corresponding to each month.

Bonds and shares whose prices are quoted in the stock exchange are adjusted by the quoted price at the end of the period, instead of by the rate of inflation. This practice is a departure from pure inflation adjustment, and problems connected with taxing capital gains that have not yet been realized may arise.

A similar problem exists concerning the treatment of foreign-exchange-denominated assets and liabilities, or those with special indexation clauses. Instead of using the rate of inflation, the exchange rate or the indexation clause is utilized to adjust the values of these assets and liabilities.

Also, a provision in Colombian law allows for the waiver of the adjustment when the market value of a nonmonetary asset is less than 50 percent of the adjusted value. This provision has little to do with inflation adjustment, and not making the adjustment in these circumstances cannot be justified.

Another provision allows the postponement of the inflation adjustment for assets that are not yet in operation. Again, this is alien to the objective of inflation adjustment, which is to tax the profits aris-

Table 13. Breakdown of the Inflation Adjustment of the 100 Largest Taxpayers, 1993

(In billions of current Colombian pesos)

Adjustment to nonmonetary assets	1,775.3
Inventories	244.2
Financial assets	215.8
Fixed assets	1,047.1
Other assets	254.4
Deferred monetary correction	13.8
Adjustment to nonmonetary liabilities	−215.8
Adjustment to deferred monetary correction	−9.1
Adjustment to net worth	−1,122.5
Adjustment to increase in net worth	−14.6
Adjustment for inflation	413.3

Sources: Division of Programming, Directorate of National Taxes; and IMF staff estimates.

ing from the inflationary erosion of the value of debt. If the asset was not financed with debt, there is no need for adjustment (either present or deferred); however, if the purchase of the asset was financed by debt, inflation is creating profits—regardless of whether the asset is already producing—and there is no reason to postpone the taxation of these profits.

Revenue Effects

A sample of the 100 biggest taxpayers (in terms of income tax paid in 1993) was used to assess the revenue effects of inflation adjustment. This sample represented almost 40 percent of the income tax revenue in that year. As Table 13 shows, an increase in the tax base of about Col$413 billion in 1993 was due to the inflation adjustment. This calculation, however, needs to be refined, as it does not recognize that depreciation allowances of adjusted assets were greater than they would have been without the adjustment of those assets' values. It was estimated that the adjustment of asset values increased depreciation allowances by about Col$82 billion (see Table 14).

Therefore, the corrected inflation adjustment amounted to about Col$331.5 billion in 1993. With a tax rate of 30 percent, this would imply an increase in tax revenues, owing to the adjustment, of about Col$100 million, or about 18 percent of the income tax revenue collected from the taxpayers in the sample. Thus, there has been no revenue loss as a result of inflation adjustment but indeed a net gain, even though, understandably, this is not consistent across all sectors.

Table 14. Corporate Income Tax: Adjustment for Inflation, Statutory Deduction, and Net Effect, 1993
(In billions of Colombian pesos)

Sector	Number of Cases	Adjustment of Nonmonetary Assets				Adjustment of Nonmonetary Liabilities and Net Worth		Adjustment for Asset Depreciation (7)	Adjustment for Inflation[1] (8)	Statutory Deduction	Net Effect[2] (10)
		Inventories (1)	Financial assets (2)	Fixed assets (3)	Other assets and adjustments to deferred monetary correction (4)	Nonmonetary liabilities and deferred monetary correction (5)	Net worth (6)				
Mining	10	63.8	38.0	718.5	73.9	81.6	348.6	59.8	404.2	98.4	305.6
Food	11	29.4	78.5	67.0	10.3	2.7	160.5	2.1	19.9	1.7	18.3
Wood, cork, and paper	2	2.3	2.3	12.2	0.5	2.0	9.7	0.4	5.2	0.2	5.0
Chemicals	18	35.3	5.3	47.9	6.8	8.1	63.2	2.7	21.3	3.2	18.1
Minerals	15	33.1	10.0	40.6	4.5	4.1	58.8	2.5	22.8	3.6	19.2
Gas and vapor	2	0.4	—	11.1	0.2	0.4	5.9	1.4	4.0	0.3	3.7
Construction	1	—	19.1	0.5	1.9	—	21.1	—	0.4	—	0.4
Wholesale commerce	7	46.0	0.2	19.8	0.6	0.2	21.4	0.8	44.2	0.6	43.6
Retail commerce	5	21.8	—	5.1	1.2	1.5	10.4	0.5	15.7	0.8	14.8
Financial	25	—	54.8	89.3	165.8	122.6	379.3	7.5	−199.5	0.6	−200.1
Services	4	12.2	7.6	35.0	2.3	1.6	58.2	4.1	−6.6	—	−6.6
Total	100	244.3	215.8	1,047.0	268.0	224.8	1,137.1	81.8	331.5	109.5	222.0

Sources: Division of Programming, Directorate of National Taxes; and IMF staff estimates.
[1](8) = (1) + (2) + (3) + (4) − (5) − (6) − (7).
[2](10) = (8) − (9).

IV Customs Tariff Reform

Introduction

In reviewing Colombia's trade policy, García García (1988) has shown that the net effect of several liberalization episodes from 1950 to the early 1980s was practically nil, as the Colombian economy in 1983 was as closed to trade as it had been in 1950, with fewer than 1 percent of tariff items importable without a license.

After the Second World War, the Colombian Government, like almost all Latin American governments, had as its goal the industrialization of the country. In the case of Colombia, this goal was pursued without doing too much harm to the agricultural sector, according to García García and Montes Llamas (1989). Trade policy during the 1950s and 1960s was characterized mainly by an export tax on coffee (justified by "optimal tariff" arguments), moderate protection for other agricultural commodities, high tariffs on consumer goods, overvalued exchange rates, and low tariffs for intermediate and capital goods.

Most Colombian industrialists had originated after the 1930s as, and continued to be, coffee growers. Wearing both hats, they wanted a high real exchange rate, and devaluation served to promote coffee exports while protecting the infant industries that produced consumer goods. With the advancement of import substitution, newly arrived industrialists with no ties to the coffee industry preferred an overvalued peso, which made imported intermediate and raw materials cheaper. The Government then faced a decision as to the "correct" price for foreign exchange. The outcome in the 1950s and 1960s was often a multiple exchange rate system and "fine-tuned" import tariff rates.

Several instruments were used in a less-than-perfect matching to attain the multiple objectives. The import tariffs of that time were intended to tax the luxury consumption of imports, according to Gillis and McLure (1971), who also point out that the sales tax was used as a supplementary means of protection through the imposition of higher rates on a number of imported products than on similar domestically produced items.

Subsequently, the industrialists became concerned about the size of the domestic market, and, after the balance of payments crisis of 1966, they were able to persuade the Government to promote exports of their products without having to be competitive in the world markets. In this way, a number of instruments of export promotion were created in the late 1960s. Credit was subsidized through a fund called "Promoción de Exportaciones" (PROEXPO),[33] Tax Reimbursement Certificates (CERTs) were granted to nontraditional exports in proportion to their f.o.b. values, and Decree No. 444 was issued in 1967, which, by allowing periodic changes in the exchange rate, created in practice a crawling peg system.

The 1984–86 economic program achieved a significant reduction in the level of tariff rates, as the average tariff fell from 61 percent to 30 percent. However, a 10 percent tariff surcharge on all tariff items was introduced in 1985 and increased to 18 percent in 1987. As reported by Hallberg and Takacs (1992), unrestricted tariff positions as a proportion of total tariff positions increased from 0.5 percent to 38 percent during the program period. The items that were liberalized, however, were mostly noncompeting inputs for locally manufactured goods, so that external competition for the domestic industry was not significantly increased.

The need for a full-fledged trade liberalization was, however, widely recognized in Colombia, and a new liberalization program was implemented in March 1990. The pace of this program was accelerated in 1991, after which, however, concerns about the resulting reduction in revenue began to emerge. This section addresses this issue and explores ways to cope with the revenue reduction that are consistent with the liberalization process.

Note: This section was prepared by Osvaldo Schenone.

[33]In 1991, PROEXPO was modified to place greater emphasis on commercial profitability of exports and was renamed PROEXPORT.

Table 15. Average Tariffs and Tariff Surcharges
(In percent)

	Number of Items	Average Tariff						Average Tariff Plus Surcharge				
		1989	1990[1]	1991	1992	1993	1994	1990[1]	1991	1992	1993	1994
Consumer goods	981	43.5	36.7	36.7	29.4	18.5	12.8	49.6	49.6	39.4	26.4	20.8
Nondurable	630	44.8	37.4	37.4	30.0	18.8	13.1	50.3	50.3	39.9	26.7	21.0
Durable	351	41.2	35.5	35.5	28.3	18.0	12.4	48.5	48.5	38.3	26.0	20.4
Raw materials/intermediates	2,928	22.9	18.8	18.8	16.1	10.3	6.0	30.9	30.9	25.5	17.8	13.5
Fuels and lubricants	34	13.7	12.1	12.1	10.6	6.9	4.3	24.7	24.7	20.3	14.7	12.0
For agriculture	115	9.4	8.4	8.4	6.5	4.7	4.0	18.1	18.1	14.7	11.9	11.1
For industry	2,779	23.6	19.4	19.4	16.6	10.6	6.0	31.5	31.5	26.0	18.1	13.6
Capital goods	1,234	22.1	14.6	14.6	10.7	6.7	4.2	27.3	27.3	20.6	16.7	12.2
Construction material	147	28.7	24.4	24.4	20.8	13.0	7.6	37.4	37.4	30.8	21.0	15.6
For agriculture	70	13.8	10.1	10.1	7.8	5.2	4.1	19.8	19.8	16.5	13.2	12.1
For industry	828	20.6	11.9	11.9	9.1	5.7	3.5	24.8	24.8	19.1	13.7	11.6
Transport equipment	189	26.3	20.4	20.4	15.4	9.4	6.6	33.3	33.3	25.4	17.4	14.6
Total	5,143	26.6	21.1	21.1	17.5	11.0	6.9	33.5	33.5	27.0	18.8	14.6

Source: Hallberg and Takacs (1992).
[1]After reforms of Decree No. 2755 of November 14, 1990.

Developments Preceding the 1991 Reform

The first phase of the trade liberalization program, which extended until mid-1991, consisted of replacing quantitative restrictions with tariffs, which had the effect of maintaining approximately the overall value of imports.

In August 1990, the newly elected Government announced its intention to accelerate the trade liberalization program of the preceding Administration. At that time, freely importable items represented 67 percent of all tariff items, and the share of quantitative restrictions in the manufacturing sector had fallen from 82 percent of domestic production to 56 percent. Finally, in November 1990, quantitative restrictions were virtually eliminated with the liberalization of all tariff positions except basic agricultural products and their derivatives, and items restricted for health and safety reasons, which comprised only 3 percent of the total.[34]

The second phase of trade liberalization, which has lasted another three-and-one-half years, consists of reducing both the level and dispersion of the tariffs. Table 15 summarizes the schedule of tariff adjustments through 1994. In March 1990, the number of tariff rates was reduced from 23 to 13; the maximum tariff was cut from 200 percent to 100 percent; the average tariff fell from 27 percent to 24 percent;

[34]Hallberg and Takacs (1992).

and the uniform tariff surcharge was reduced to 16 percent. By September 1990, the average tariff and the tariff surcharge were down to 22 percent and 13 percent, respectively.

In November 1990, further tariff adjustments were made to bring the average tariff, including surcharge, to 33.5 percent. In the same month, the Government announced a schedule of tariff cuts through 1994. It was envisaged that, by that time, there would be only four tariff rates (5 percent, 10 percent, 15 percent, and, for automobiles, 50 percent), and the average tariff and tariff surcharge would be 7 percent and 8 percent, respectively.

August 1991 Tariff Reform

Early Implementation of the Tariff Reform

The most important event for trade policy in 1991 was the issuance of Decrees No. 2095 and 2096 in August. The first decree moved forward the tariff reductions originally scheduled for early 1994, and the second lowered the tariff surcharge.

This part of Section IV focuses on (1) the levels and dispersion of nominal tariffs before and after the reform; (2) the new role of surcharges after the reform; (3) the reduction in the level of effective protection; and (4) the impact of the tariff reform on collections and the possibility of reducing exemptions, so as to cope with the negative effects on receipts.

Tariffs Before and After Decree No. 2095

Both the previous tariff schedule and the new one ranged between zero percent and 75 percent. The greater concentration of tariff items around the lower tariffs is undoubtedly the most important feature of the new schedule. Of 6,847 tariff items, only 1,820 were left unchanged, while all the others were reduced.

Thus, the average tariff (weighted by the number of tariff items) was reduced from 17.34 percent to 6.61 percent, and the variance in the distribution of tariffs was lowered from 163 to 58. Chart 2 shows the difference between the previous tariff schedule and the schedule in effect following the issuance of Decree No. 2095. Under the new schedule, 98 percent of the items have tariffs of 15 percent or less, while 2 percent have tariffs ranging from 20 percent to 75 percent. These higher rates have been applied to a few agricultural commodities and to automobiles, pickup trucks, and campers.

The zero percent tariff is applicable to raw materials, capital goods, and a few articles easily brought into Colombia illegally (such as liquor, cigarettes, and certain household appliances that are not produced locally). Raw materials that are produced nationally have a 5 percent tariff, which is not applicable to other goods.[35] Under Decree No. 2095, 1,162 tariff items that had been subject to higher rates have been reduced to the 5 percent level.

As a result, tariff items at rates of zero percent to 5 percent account for 60 percent of the total items in the customs tariff. The 10 percent tariff, which has been applied to capital goods produced nationally and to pharmaceuticals, covers 17 percent of all tariff items. Decree No. 2095 has transferred to this level 1,173 items that had previously been subject to tariffs of more than 10 percent.

The 15 percent tariff is applicable to all final consumer goods that are produced locally and to vehicles for transporting passengers and freight. This rate applies to 21 percent of all tariff items. Under Decree No. 2095, 1,328 items that had previously had higher tariffs have been moved to this tariff level.

Surcharges Before and After Decree No. 2096

The 9 tax levels in effect after August 1991 increase to 14 when the surcharges of zero percent, 5 percent, and 8 percent are taken into account. Of these 14 levels, however, 93 percent of tariff items are concentrated in 4 levels—at rates of 8 percent, 13 percent, 18 percent, and 23 percent—as indicated in Chart 3.

---

[35]The only exception is weapons, for which the only authorized importer is the Ministry of Defense.

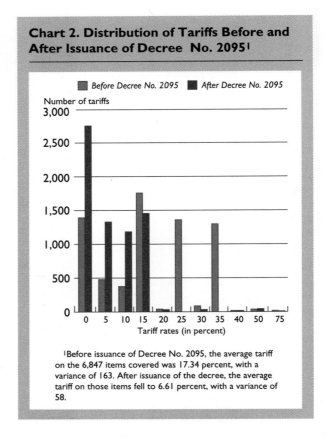

Chart 2. Distribution of Tariffs Before and After Issuance of Decree No. 2095[1]

Before Decree No. 2095 — After Decree No. 2095

Number of tariffs

Tariff rates (in percent)

[1]Before issuance of Decree No. 2095, the average tariff on the 6,847 items covered was 17.34 percent, with a variance of 163. After issuance of the decree, the average tariff on those items fell to 6.61 percent, with a variance of 58.

It should be noted that, even though the surcharges extend the range of tariff values from zero percent to 83 percent (compared with the previous range of zero percent to 75 percent), there is a greater concentration of rates as a result of the surcharges. Basically, application of the surcharges has caused the extreme value of zero percent to virtually disappear. Thus, the average tariff rate (weighted by the number of tariff positions) rises from 6.61 percent to 14.18 percent with the inclusion of surcharges, (see Chart 3), but the variances are virtually identical, at 58 and 55, respectively (see Charts 2 and 3).

Impact on Effective Protection

The above findings indicate that surcharges increase the average value of total taxes on imports without increasing their dispersion. The result is an overall tariff structure with higher receipts and less dispersion of effective protection among the various sectors of the economy, as shown in Table 16. A number of interesting conclusions might be derived from this table.

First, the effective protection provided by tariffs alone is less than what it was prior to issuance of Decree No. 2095. As a consequence of the decree,

Chart 3. Distribution of Taxation, With and Without Surcharges, After Issuance of Decree No. 2095[1]

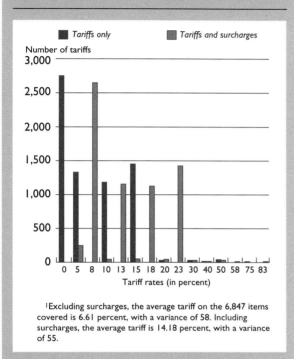

[1]Excluding surcharges, the average tariff on the 6,847 items covered is 6.61 percent, with a variance of 58. Including surcharges, the average tariff is 14.18 percent, with a variance of 55.

protection ranges from 4.41 percent to 35.24 percent, whereas it previously ranged from 7.06 percent to 60.79 percent (see columns (2) and (1), respectively, of Table 16).

Second, the effective protection generated by the tariff schedule and surcharges together is less than it was prior to the August 1991 reform. Protection ranges from 11.26 percent to 48.20 percent, whereas it previously ranged from 12.68 percent to 78.18 percent (see columns (4) and (3), respectively, of Table 16). Moreover, the dispersion of effective protection is also reduced: the ratio of maximum to minimum effective protection declined from 6.2 (that is, 78.18/12.68) to 4.3 (48.2/11.26).

Finally, although the effective protection generated after the reform by the sum of tariffs and surcharges is greater than that generated by only tariffs, the dispersion is less (see columns (4) and (2) of Table 16). Taking tariffs alone, effective protection for the various sectors ranges from 4.41 percent to 35.24 percent (with the maximum value eight times greater than the minimum) while, with surcharges factored in, effective protection ranges from 11.26 percent to 48.20 percent (with the maximum value only 4.3 times greater than the minimum). These findings indicate that, by reducing the average effec-

tive protection and dispersion, the tariff reform encourages a more efficient allocation of resources.

The reduction in effective protection should also reduce the antiexport bias. By reducing the incentives that made sales in the protected domestic market artificially attractive, exports (which suffered from a comparative disadvantage) have been rendered less unattractive. This reduction, in turn, points to the lack of justification for continuing to grant CERTs, as the reason for establishing them was precisely to offset the antiexport bias.[36]

The amounts of CERTs granted rose consistently, from Col$45.4 billion in 1989 to Col$68.6 billion in 1990 and to Col$52.9 billion for the first eight months of 1991, as indicated in Appendix VI. Between the first half of 1990 and the first half of 1991, the amount of CERTs granted increased by 20 percent, while the value of nontraditional exports rose by 90 percent (from US$1.1 billion to US$2.1 billion).[37] The value of CERTs per Colombian peso of exports thus went down during this time. The reduction of the antiexport bias that inevitably occurred as a result of the August 1991 reform argues in favor of even greater cutbacks in the amount of the CERTs. In turn, this move would have a favorable effect on the public finances, as it would help offset the fiscal impact of the reform.

Cost and Financing of Faster Trade Liberalization

There are two ways to estimate the effects of faster trade liberalization on revenues: first, the so-called aggregate procedure, based on macroeconomic projections of GDP, imports, and receipts; and second, the tariff item procedure, based on simulations of the price elasticities of demand for tariff items or groups of items.

Aggregate Procedure

Table 17 presents two aggregate estimations—by the National Planning Department and the Ministry of Finance, respectively—for 1991 and 1992, the years in which the accelerated economic opening could have had a significant fiscal impact.[38] Table 17

---

[36]It might be recalled that CERTs are granted for nontraditional exports in proportion to their f.o.b. value at rates of 3 percent, 6 percent, 9 percent, or 12 percent, depending on the product in question and the country to which it is being exported. CERTs are freely negotiable on the stock exchange and are accepted at par value in payment of taxes.

[37]Since the nominal exchange rate went up during this period, the increase in these exports, when expressed in Colombian pesos, was even greater than 90 percent.

[38]In 1993, the tariffs and surcharges would have been approximately the same, and, for 1994, they would have been identical, with or without the accelerated opening.

Table 16. **Effective Protection by Use or Economic Purpose of Goods, Before and After Issuance of Decree No. 2095**
(In percent)

		Tariff		Tariff plus Surcharge	
Category	Number of NANDINA[1] Items	Before Decree No. 2095 (1)	After Decree No. 2095 (2)	Before Decree No. 2095 (3)	After Decree No. 2095 (4)
Consumer goods	1,625	60.37	31.54	77.34	44.99
Nondurables	1,066	60.79	29.60	78.18	43.31
Durables	559	59.58	35.24	75.74	48.20
Raw materials and intermediate inputs	3,441	30.49	10.57	44.19	21.35
Fuels and lubricants	38	25.85	12.70	41.41	25.15
Agricultural raw materials	112	34.68	31.35	39.39	35.99
Industrial raw materials	3,291	30.40	9.84	44.38	21.00
Capital goods	1,764	14.18	6.76	28.09	18.03
Construction materials	246	34.77	12.90	50.10	25.16
Agricultural capital goods	79	7.06	4.76	12.68	11.26
Industrial capital goods	1,179	8.45	4.41	22.66	15.86
Transportation equipment	260	22.83	12.18	36.57	23.21
Other	17	22.52	17.43	37.26	29.20
Total	6,847	33.36	14.58	47.89	26.22

Source: Ministry of Finance.
[1]"Normas del Pacto Andino" (NANDINA) provides the basis—the definition of products via a common eight-digit nomenclature—for the harmonization of the common external tariff of the Andean Pact countries.

assumes that the taxes—whether tariffs, surcharges, or the value-added tax (VAT)—actually collected (that is, discounting exemptions and tax evasion) represented the same percentage of theoretical receipts that would have been collected without the accelerated opening of the economy. These results, however, might overestimate the drop in receipts, because the percentage of effectiveness of taxation might increase (instead of remaining constant) under the more open economy, as the incentive to evade taxes or lobby to obtain exemptions—or both—should drop with the reduction in tariffs and surcharges.

Both the National Planning Department and the Ministry of Finance estimated a fiscal cost of Col$184 billion for 1992; however, for 1991, the National Planning Department estimated a fiscal cost that was nearly Col$80 billion higher (Col$85 billion versus Col$6 billion).

Tariff Item Procedure

The estimations described above did not consider the influence of the composition of imports on the response to tariff changes. Hence, an alternative methodology was developed that takes into account the different demand elasticities of each group of imports.

The impact on receipts of reducing taxes on a product depends basically on the price elasticity of the demand for that product. The formula that computes this impact, as developed in Appendix VI, is as follows:

$$dRec = CIF \left(\frac{-Nt_1}{1 + t_0} - 1 \right) (t_0 - t_1),$$

where *dRec* is the change in receipts collected, *CIF* is the initial value of imports of the product at the international price, *N* is the price elasticity of demand for the product, t_0 is the initial taxation (tariff + surcharge), and t_1 is the final taxation (tariff + surcharge).

The computation was done for each of the 4,700 tariff items for which there were imports. The tariff items were grouped into 16 categories. The estimation procedure is described in Appendix VI, and Table 37 in that appendix presents the results. The greatest losses in collections were experienced by chemical products and tools and machinery, which totaled a revenue loss for 1992 of between Col$209 billion (based on "pessimistic" assump-

Table 17. Estimations of the Fiscal Cost of Accelerated Opening by the National Planning Department (PLAN) and Ministry of Finance (FIN)
(In billions of current Colombian pesos)

| | 1991 | | 1991 Accelerated | | 1992 | | 1992 Accelerated | | Fiscal Cost of Accelerated Opening | | | |
| | | | | | | | | | 1991 | | 1992 | |
	PLAN (1)	FIN (2)	PLAN (3)	FIN (4)	PLAN (5)	FIN (6)	PLAN (7)	FIN (8)	PLAN (1)–(3)	FIN (2)–(4)	PLAN (5)–(7)	FIN (6)–(8)
Tariff	233	205.0	180	184.5	282	274	149	163.0	53	20.5	133	111.0
Surcharge	276	276.8	250	266.1	310	300	256	248.2	26	10.7	54	51.8
VAT	311	307.1	305	332.0	439	429	441	408.0	6	−24.9	−2	21.0
Total	820	788.9	734	782.6	1,030	1,003	846	819.2	85	6.3	185	183.8

Sources: National Planning Department; and Ministry of Finance.

tions) and Col\$175 billion (based on "optimistic" assumptions).[39]

The concern associated with the fiscal cost of the accelerated opening of the economy raises questions about the source of the needed financing. These are legitimate questions and should not be interpreted as criticism of the decision to accelerate the opening; it is to be expected that implementing an economic policy that is preferable to the previous one comes at a cost. A way of dealing with the fiscal cost in a manner consistent with Colombia's current foreign trade policy would be to reduce exemptions from the tariff, surcharge, and VAT on imports—singly or in combination—as is analyzed below.

A Complementary Policy

Another simulation exercise consistent with Colombia's prevailing foreign trade policy was carried out, in which the surcharge was made uniform at 8 percent, in order to deal with the fiscal cost of the accelerated opening of the economy. This exercise was not envisaged as an alternative to a substantial reduction in exemptions, as it would have the greatest impact on receipts and the efficiency of resource allocation. Rather, the formula represented a policy compatible with openness, as it tended to make taxes more uniform. In fact, the 14 levels of taxes (ranging between zero percent and 83 percent) shown in Chart 3 were reduced under the formula to 8 levels (ranging between 8 percent and 83 percent). This simulation exercise resulted in the tax distribution shown in Chart 4, with a variance more or less equal to that

shown in Chart 3—59, as against 55—and with a slightly higher average tax rate (weighted by the number of items) of 14.5 percent, compared with the existing rate of 14.2 percent.

Average taxation (weighted by the value of imports) was substantially higher under this exercise, which, if implemented, could have alleviated in part the fiscal cost of the August 1991 reform. Recalculating the values of Table 37 in Appendix VI by incorporating a uniform 8 percent surcharge resulted (Table 38, Appendix VI) in a 20 percent reduction in the fiscal cost. It is more efficient to increase the surcharges of less than 8 percent to 8 percent than to increase the tariffs by an equivalent amount, because the exemption arrangements for surcharges tend to be stricter, making them an instrument more consistent with the principle of uniform taxation. Also, the impact on tax collections of the increased surcharges should be more reliable, even while the exemptions are being reduced.

An Alternative Complementary Policy

While the reduction of exemptions (the primary approach to dealing with the fiscal cost incurred as a result of the opening of the economy) was generating more receipts and making the tax treatment of imports more uniform, the impact of that action could have been strengthened by taking two complementary measures: unifying the surcharges at a single rate, as already mentioned; and reducing the share of CERTs granted for exports.

With effective protection having been lowered by the reduction in tariffs and surcharges, sales on the domestic market had become less attractive. Meanwhile, the same liberalization of imports had automatically made exports (for which there had been

---

[39]The estimate of the National Planning Department and the Finance Ministry—Col\$186 billion—fell between these two assumptions.

Chart 4. Distribution of Taxation Using Current and Uniform Surcharges[1]

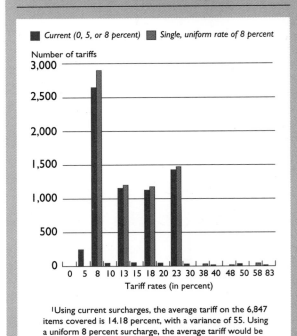

■ Current (0, 5, or 8 percent)   ■ Single, uniform rate of 8 percent

Number of tariffs

[1]Using current surcharges, the average tariff on the 6,847 items covered is 14.18 percent, with a variance of 55. Using a uniform 8 percent surcharge, the average tariff would be 14.46 percent, with a variance of 59.

Table 18. Effective Rates of Customs Taxes
(In percent)

	Tariffs	Surcharge	VAT
1986	12.1	11.5	7.5
1987	11.7	13.2	7.6
1988	11.3	12.8	8.0
1989	9.8	12.6	7.6
1990	7.6	10.8	6.9
1991[1]	7.2	8.9	7.6

Source: Ministry of Finance.
[1]Through June 1991.

little incentive) more attractive. That is to say, the antiexport bias had been reduced with the effective reduction in protection.

This reduction, in turn, would have made it possible to take the complementary measure of reducing the percentages of CERTs granted for exports, as their raison d'être had been precisely to offset the antiexport bias. Assuming a reduction in the amount of CERTs by at least one third from a 1991 base figure of Col$75 billion (see Table 39, Appendix VI), it would have been possible to recover an amount more or less equal to the amount lost by unifying the surcharges, namely, about Col$25-Col$30 billion, at 1992 prices.

Treatment of Exemptions to Tariffs, Surcharges, and the VAT

It was found by the staff that the ratio of actual customs receipts to the c.i.f. value of imports was substantially lower than the tax percentage applicable under law. This clearly showed that exemptions were widespread. There must also have been some evasion.[40] Table 18 shows the effective tariff, sur-

charge, and VAT rates applied to imports during 1986–91.

The amount of import exemptions was quite sizable: during the first half of 1991, receipts from tariffs, surcharges, and the VAT (Col$365 billion) barely exceeded the amount of exemptions from these taxes (Col$334 billion).

A sampling of exemptions granted by 10 customs offices (out of the 18 in the country) for the period August–December 1990 was obtained.[41] A comparison with the exemptions granted by these 10 customs offices during the period January–May 1991 revealed that the amount of exemptions increased during that period by over 50 percent in nominal terms, from Col$59 billion to Col$91 billion. As imports increased during the period by less than 50 percent in nominal terms, the conclusion could be drawn that effective tax rates dropped between August–December 1990 and January–May 1991 at the customs offices in the sample.

This result from the sampling of 10 customs offices suggests that the decline in the real rate of taxation observed in Table 18 is not attributable solely to the reductions in tariff and surcharge rates that occurred during the August 1990 to May 1991 period, but also to an increase in exemptions. If this sample can be taken as representative of the overall situation, it must also be noted that the increase in exemptions in relation to the amount of imports is not consistent with the assumptions regarding collections mentioned above. Nor is it compatible with a foreign trade policy designed to promote competitiveness through more uniform and less distortion-

---

[40]The most common form of tax evasion, the underinvoicing of imports, is not included in the indicator mentioned because it

simultaneously reduces both receipts and the declared c.i.f. value (that is, the numerator and denominator of the ratio to be compared with the legal rates).

[41]These customs offices are located in Cúcuta, Ipiales, Buenaventura, Bogotá, Cali, Manizales, Medellín, San Andrés, Turbo, and Bucaramanga.

Table 19. Collections, Exemptions, and Imports at All Customhouses, January–June 1991
(In billions of Colombian pesos, unless otherwise specified)

	Import Value c.i.f.		Value of Exemptions (3)	Collections (4)	(4)/[(1) + (2)]	(3)/(1)	(3)/[(1) + (2)]
	With some exemptions (1)	With no exemptions (2)			(In percent)		
January	72.5	137.1	58.9	49.3	23.5	81.2	28.1
February	104.9	150.9	85.9	58.1	22.7	81.9	33.6
March	71.6	138.4	64.1	53.7	25.6	89.5	30.5
April	66.0	178.9	55.1	65.3	26.7	83.5	22.5
May	78.2	196.0	39.9	71.3	26.0	51.0	14.6
June	68.3	192.2	30.2	67.0	25.7	44.2	11.6
January–June	461.5	993.5	334.1	364.7	25.1	72.4	23.0

Source: IMF staff estimates.

ary taxes, which in general requires fewer exemptions and other preferential approaches.

Examining this subject in greater detail—and bearing in mind that the objective of foreign trade policy requires the reduction of exemptions—raises two questions. First, how were the exemptions distributed among tariffs, surcharges, and the VAT? Second, what was the breakdown among, respectively, the exemptions that were justified for reasons of economic efficiency, such as for duty-free inputs to produce exportable goods under the Vallejo Plan;[42] those required by virtue of international commitments, including the Latin American Integration Association (LAIA) and the Andean Pact; and those granted for other reasons?

In 1991, 32 different legal provisions granted tax exemptions. Ten provided for exemption from payment of all three taxes, and the remaining 22 provided for exemption from payment of one or two taxes. The VAT was subject to the fewest exemptions, as 13 legal provisions exempted imports from that tax. Meanwhile, 18 provisions exempted imports from surcharges, and 25 provisions (80 percent of the total of 32) exempted them from tariff payments, as indicated in Table 40, Appendix VI. Of a total of Col$334 billion in exemptions granted during the first half of 1991, nearly one half were tariff exemp-

tions, and nearly one third were exemptions from the VAT, with the remainder composed of exemptions from surcharges. Staff calculations further indicated that, during the same period, one third of all imports were exempt from either the tariff, the surcharge, the VAT, or some combination thereof.

Table 19 shows that customs receipts from all sources ranged between 23 percent and 27 percent of the c.i.f. value of imports during the first six months of 1991. These percentages represent the weighted-average tax for each peso of imports (including all imports, even those that were completely exempt). The last column of this table also shows that the fiscal sacrifice (the value of the exemptions) declined from about 30 percent of the c.i.f. value of imports at the start of the year to almost 11 percent in June. These percentages represent the weighted average exemption for each peso of imports (including all imports, even those that received no exemptions).

Of greater interest is what Table 19 shows in the penultimate column. The value of exemptions as a percent of the value of imports subject to exemption declined from between 80 percent and 90 percent at the beginning of 1991 to 44 percent in June. These figures suggest that the imports enjoying exemption were precisely those that would have been subject to the highest taxes (especially during January–April 1991). This hypothesis, in turn, suggests that the majority of these exemptions did not apply to the raw materials used to produce exports, as specified under the Vallejo Plan.

More specifically, according to the above-mentioned sample of 10 customs offices, imports under special arrangements, such as the Vallejo Plan, accounted for 43 percent of total exemptions from August 1990 to May 1991, while diplomatic imports

---

[42]The Vallejo Plan (named after the Minister who proposed it—Vallejo Arbelaez) was introduced in 1959 as an import duty drawback scheme, aimed at promoting the growth of nontraditional exports (as opposed to the main traditional exports of coffee, coal, gold, and petroleum).

The Vallejo Plan reduced the cost of imported inputs (intermediate and capital goods) for producers of nontraditional exports through the issuance of CERTs against import duties paid, which were accepted as payment for taxes. CERTs continue in use, but their rates have been substantially reduced.

or imports under the Andean Pact and LAIA accounted for 30 percent of total exemptions. In other words, 73 percent of the exemptions in the sample were made because of international treaties or to maintain the competitiveness of exports. The remaining 27 percent of exemptions, totaling about Col$40 billion for the period under review, could therefore have been eliminated before the others.

It should also be noted that this estimate was constructed from a sampling of 10 customs offices over a 10-month period. If all 18 customs offices were considered for a period of 12 months, the estimate would be substantially higher than Col$40 billion. By extending the period of the sample from 10 months to one year, by assuming that the exemptions were distributed uniformly over the year, and by taking into account the fact that the eight customhouses not covered by the sample (which include large customhouses in Barranquilla and Cartagena) granted exemptions over the 10-month period that were almost twice as large as those granted by the 10 customhouses in the sample,[43] it may be concluded that the exemptions that could have been eliminated amounted to more than Col$140 billion at 1991 prices, or Col$164 billion at 1992 prices.

Even if the authorities had been able to effectively eliminate only one half of these exemptions (for instance, those extended to San Andrés—a "zona franca," in which imports are sold duty free to domestic consumers—and to the mining sector, as well as those granted by resolutions and miscellaneous, unclassified exemptions), the amounts collected would be sufficient to recover in two or three years the fiscal cost of the accelerated opening of the economy, which has been estimated in this section at between Col$175 billion and Col$209 billion in 1992. In subsequent years, the elimination of exemptions would continue to produce additional receipts while generating a less discriminatory protective structure, which would further the development of the economy's more competitive activities.

Summing Up

By advancing the tariff and surcharge reductions originally scheduled for January 1994 to August 1991, a fiscal cost was incurred in terms of the significant decrease in 1992 collections. The fiscal cost in 1991 was limited and for the most part inevitable. It was limited because the reform occurred in August and therefore affected only the receipts for the last quarter of 1991. Moreover, the fiscal cost in 1993 was not high; even if the reductions had not been moved

forward, taxes on trade in 1993 would already have been very close to their post-reform levels. The estimates made by staff quantified this 1992 cost at Col$175–Col$209 billion (at 1992 prices), a level consistent with the Col$185–Col$186 billion estimated on the basis of macroeconomic methods by the National Planning Department and the Ministry of Finance.

This raises the question of how this fiscal cost could have best been financed. This is a legitimate question; it should not be interpreted as a criticism of the accelerated opening of the economy, because adopting an economic policy that is better than the previous one cannot and should not be expected to be accomplished at zero cost. Dealing with this fiscal cost in a manner consistent with Colombia's current foreign trade policy would have entailed reducing the exemptions to tariffs, surcharges, and the VAT on imports—singly or in combination. Exemptions, in fact, were concentrated more on tariffs than on surcharges or the VAT. During the first half of 1991, the fiscal sacrifice of the three exemptions came to Col$334 billion (of which nearly one half represented tariff exemptions), which was virtually the same amount as the revenue from tariffs, surcharges, and the VAT for the same period (Col$365 billion).

Some of these exemptions were needed to preserve the competitiveness of exports—for example, the exemptions of imported inputs used in the production of exports under the Vallejo Plan—so it was probably not advisable to eliminate them. There were also the exemptions that existed by virtue of international treaties, such as for imports under the Andean Pact or the LAIA, or those granted for diplomatic reasons. Nevertheless, many of the exemptions could have been abolished. The sampling of the ten customs offices mentioned above indicates that about Col$40 billion in exemptions were granted for reasons other than the Vallejo Plan or international agreements. These exemptions could probably have been eliminated relatively quickly and easily.

In addition to reducing exemptions, another complementary way of dealing with the fiscal cost of the accelerated opening of the economy—which would have been consistent with Colombia's trade policy—would have been to establish a uniform surcharge of 8 percent to replace the current three rates of zero percent, 5 percent, and 8 percent. It was estimated that making the surcharge rate uniform at 8 percent would have made it possible to recover approximately 20 percent of the fiscal cost of the accelerated opening in 1992. Moreover, its favorable impact on receipts and its contribution to economic efficiency would have lasted beyond 1992.

The elimination of CERTs would have constituted another measure to deal with the fiscal cost of the accelerated opening. Nontraditional exports (that is,

---

[43]As indicated above, of a total exemption of Col$334 billion in 1991, the sample accounted for only Col$91 billion.

exports other than coffee, untanned hides, or petroleum and its by-products) receive CERTs in an amount determined by their exported values. CERTs, however, could be eliminated completely on the grounds that their purpose—to reduce the antiexport bias—is better served by accelerating the liberalization process.

The main lesson to be drawn from the discussions on tariff reform is that the Government's urgency to secure revenue did not conflict with the adoption of policies designed to enhance resource allocation efficiency. The measures considered would have simultaneously promoted efficiency and yielded increased revenue.

V Conclusions and Future Directions for Reform

Colombia has been engaged in a continuous tax reform effort over the decades, with each reform comprising some improvement in the tax structure. The major reform measures of the 1990s have reflected the opening up and modernization of the economy. This section reviews the progress that has been made in the areas of customs tariffs, income taxes, value-added tax (VAT), tax indexation, and tax incentives, and considers the direction of future reform efforts in Colombia.

Customs Tariff Reform

Historically, the approach of Colombia's governments to trade policy was characterized by a heavy emphasis on protectionism, particularly for industrial products. Indeed, for a considerable period of time, the simple promise to create a new import-substitute industry was sufficient for the authorities to guarantee its owners that, once domestic production was initiated, all imports of similar merchandise would be prohibited. Tariff rates were high, on average, and extended over a wide range. Moreover, the actual level of protection often exceeded that accorded by the tariff structure as such, through the use of prior licenses and a prohibited list.

Now, at the final stages of the customs tariff reform, the prevailing structure of tariffs (0–40 percent) is a vast improvement over the structures prevailing in Colombia during the past decade, and even more over those prevailing in the 1960s and 1970s. This structure narrows greatly the degree of variation in nominal tariff rates and, obviously, the rates of effective protection.

Currently, the highest "important" rate of tariff in Colombia is 20 percent. (Motorized vehicles carry higher rates, of 35 percent and 40 percent.) At the 20 percent rate, there are 1,549 tariff positions, mostly covering final consumer products. At the same time, there are 162 products carrying a zero tariff, and 2,575 products carrying a 5 percent tariff. Thus, despite the customs tariff reform, there could still be

thousands of cases in which different operations within one category use vastly different proportions of imported inputs that are taxed at different rates.[44]

Another point of considerable importance is the treatment of imported capital goods within the tariff structure. There is a widespread tendency in the developing world to give preferential treatment to imports of capital equipment, especially when they do not compete with similar equipment produced at home. It seems natural to think that, by putting a tariff on such capital goods, a government is only interfering with the efficient making of the final products that use those capital goods. However, that conclusion should not be arrived at too hastily.

To think through this problem, society's objectives in instituting a protective tariff in the first place must be kept in mind. These objectives can be formulated in three ways that are compatible with a general tariff policy. (Other objectives, such as defense, exploiting monopsony power in world markets, and compensating for certain domestic distortions, lead to the imposition of tariffs focused on particular products or areas, but not to general tariffs.)

It can be said that one objective of a generalized tariff policy is to assign a higher cost to the use of foreign exchange than to its production. The end result of pursuing this objective is to equalize, in all different uses and lines of production, the value of domestic resources devoted to saving one dollar of foreign exchange. Stating the objective in this way makes it clear that a firm using imported capital inputs and a firm using imported current inputs ought to be put on an equal footing. Thus, a uniform tariff rate should be applied to imports of capital goods, as well as to those of current inputs and final products.

Consider, for example, a firm whose output is subject to a 20 percent tariff and whose current imported inputs amount to 50 percent of the international price of the product. If those inputs were allowed to enter

---

Note: This section was prepared by Arnold C. Harberger.

[44]Perhaps a local firm produces compressors for refrigerators, but only of certain sizes. Compressors for different-sized refrigerators would then have to be imported. The same situation applies for all kinds of inputs into production, such as motors, sensors, and chemicals.

duty free, that firm would be encouraged to use up to Col\$1,120 of Colombian resources in order to save one dollar of foreign exchange (assuming a market exchange rate of Col\$800 to the dollar).

Now consider a counterpart firm, which imports no capital equipment but has interest and depreciation costs (on foreign-made capital equipment) that likewise amount to one half of the international price of the product. It is quite fair for the authorities to treat those interest and depreciation costs as if they were current dollar outlays because the purchase price of a capital asset will, in equilibrium, be equal to the present value of its future flow of gross return to capital (net return plus depreciation). This is true of every asset when its internal rate of return is used as the discount rate, and of assets yielding the normal rate of return when the latter is used as the discount rate.

A second objective of a generalized tariff treatment is to give an equal degree of protection to all sorts of import-substituting domestic activities. In this context, the key issue is whether the value added that accrues to imported capital equipment should be categorized as "domestic value added." Is this part of what should be protected, or is it an ancillary cost (similar to that of an imported current input) of undertaking the activities that are being protected? Treating the services of imported capital equipment as an ancillary cost—directly analogous to the costs of other imported inputs—is clearly one way to justify the imposition of a uniform tariff aimed at providing equal protection to import-substituting activities.

A third way of thinking about the institution of a protective tariff is to take an explicitly short- or medium-term view, in which all capital in place is considered to be "domestic capital," in the same sense that GDP measures something called "domestic product." From this viewpoint, the earnings of domestic capital are considered as simply an economic rent to the existing stock of assets. The machines are viewed as capable of being sold from one industry or activity to another, and the buildings and even land as capable of being occupied and utilized by one activity or another. Naturally, the various types and skills of labor can be used in many different activities throughout the economy and can be shifted from one sector to another.

This way of looking at the situation puts the return to domestic capital and land on a par with the return to labor. In this context, imposition of a 20 percent uniform tariff declares a willingness to use up to 20 percent more domestic resources to produce capital goods or current inputs locally than to import them from abroad, or to produce an equivalent number of dollars' worth of output via the export route.

These three justifications of a generalized protec-

tive tariff are compatible with each other, although the compatibility might not be readily apparent. The old economic maxim that "sunk costs are sunk" sheds some light on the situation. In the present context, this means that the foreign currency costs of the imported capital yet to come should be cause for concern, but not the costs of the capital that has already been imported. For the latter, "the die has been cast" (even if the capital goods are still being paid for). For the former, that is, the capital goods that are not yet here, foreign currency will be used to import them, and, in that sense, their foreign currency costs should be treated like those of current imported inputs. With respect to the protection of (actual or potential) domestic value added, the productivity of the foreign machinery that is already in place is domestic value added, and thus to be protected, while the entry of foreign equipment to compete with what has already been installed is a component of what must be protected against. Foreign machinery is "the enemy" as long as it is outside the home country's borders, but it becomes not just a friend, but part of the home country once it comes inside.

The level of effective protection in Colombia is still not low, despite the trade liberalization. Reflecting the arguments made above, the final step in tariff reform would be to introduce a uniform tariff. The process of establishing a uniform tariff could begin with further reductions in the level and dispersion of import duties.[45] On the export side, CERTs might be abolished, as the objective of reducing the antiexport bias has already been achieved.

The Income Tax on Juridical Persons

Integration with the Tax on Natural Persons

Colombia has made considerable strides in the taxation of income in recent years. By the beginning of the 1990s, the top marginal tax rate for natural persons and the corporate income tax rate had been equalized at 30 percent.[46] Another important step in this direction came with the elimination of double taxation. The two taxes are fully integrated as far as dividends are concerned, because taxes are levied at the source of undistributed profits. Under this system, firms paying out all their earnings in dividends

---

[45]In Latin America, Chile is currently the only country with a uniform tariff (of 11 percent). In the past, the Chilean authorities had changed the tariff rate based on revenue and other needs, but they have maintained a uniform rate since the early 1980s.

[46]Even as late as 1986, the highest marginal rate of the personal income tax was 49 percent, while the corporate income tax rate was 40 percent. Currently, a temporary surtax exists, but is planned to be eliminated in 1997.

pay a corporate income tax of 37.5 percent (including surtax), and the taxpayer pays no tax on the dividends received. Considered as an integrated tax, therefore, individual shareholders pay a 37.5 percent tax on the income generating their dividends, independent of their personal marginal income tax rate.

Colombia's treatment of dividends is prudent in the context of revenue productivity. Another method would be, for example, the typical European procedure of allowing taxpayers to take as a tax credit (akin to withholding) an amount equal to the tax rate (37.5 percent in this case) times the dividend received. With this procedure, however, the government keeps a fraction—the square of the tax rate—of the total income generated at the corporate level. (In the case of Colombia, the figure would be 9/64, or about 14 percent.)

Colombia's system of taxing dividends is also prudent in comparison with what some might consider the ideal treatment of simply allowing the corporate income to be passed through to shareholders, with the shareholders declaring their share of the corporation's income (or loss) and paying tax thereon. This "ideal" treatment sounds clear and transparent, but it creates a mare's nest of administrative problems. For example, dealing with shares of stock that are sold one or more times during a year presents formidable obstacles. The fortunes of the corporation may have taken a 180-degree turn in September, say, with significant losses occurring before that month and huge profits after. A prorated sharing of the year's profits could unjustly penalize the shareholder who sold the stock for a lower price in August. In any event, an attempt to pinpoint the actual profits accruing to the firm during the term in which each shareholder held stock could be an accounting nightmare.

Colombia's decision to abolish the capital gains tax on shares is also interesting. This decision can be justified on economic grounds. First, it should be noted that there is an economic connection between a company's real reinvested earnings and the real capital gains on its outstanding shares. Although this connection is far from exact, it is based on what would occur if newly invested capital yielded a normal rate of return and if stock prices were set in the market using that normal rate of return as the capitalization rate. Significant differences between real reinvested earnings and real capital gains occur primarily when the rate of profit on investments is significantly different (in either direction) from the rate of capitalization, and when the rate of capitalization prevailing in the market as a whole undergoes significant changes. Both these variations can go in either direction, so there is no clear-cut and obvious bias involved in leaving such benefits untaxed as personal income.

Second, it can be argued that, when the rate of return on investment differs from the rate of capitalization, the treatment is quite "correct," in the sense that tax is always paid on the income that is generated within the corporation. No special justification can be made for not taxing the gains resulting from changes in the rate of capitalization, other than that no troublesome incentive effects are generated by leaving such windfall gains and losses unrecognized as far as the individual income tax is concerned.[47]

Dealing with Evasion

Administering income taxes on business firms is never easy. Colombia has made great strides in recent years by devising a practical strategy for addressing tax evasion by concentrating attention on a subgroup of relatively large taxpayers. However, that does not mean that the problem of evasion has been completely solved. In this connection, it may be useful to point out the relative success that has been obtained, both in Mexico and in Argentina, by implementing a so-called assets tax. (Peru and Ecuador have also recently introduced the tax.) The objective of this paper is only to outline the key features of the assets tax, which, however, is worthy of study—including a close consultation with tax administrators from countries using the tax.

The motivation for using an assets tax comes from both the fact of direct evasion and the possibility that firms are still benefiting from concessions and loopholes that may have unwisely been given in the past. Colombia may not suffer significantly from the latter problem, but the problem of evasion is still serious, especially outside the large-taxpayer group.

The basic idea behind the assets tax is to impute a kind of minimum income that can be expected from fixed assets. Clearly, an adequate indexing system must actually be in place to measure these assets. In Mexico's case, the tax is 2 percent of assets, which can be credited against the income tax. Thus, if a firm has an income tax liability equal to 3 percent of assets, its total tax burden is left unchanged by the assets tax. However, if a firm has an income tax liability equal to only 1 percent of its assets, it has to pay an additional 1 percent of assets in order to meet its full obligations.

Most public finance economists consider the assets tax to be a tough—but ultimately quite reasonable—way of handling the problem of evasion at the juridical-persons level. Given that real rates of return of 10 percent, 15 percent, and even 20 percent are likely to be quite normal in countries such as Colombia, income tax payments equal to between

---

[47]Examples are the recent gains produced as the general rate of capitalization in Colombia's stock market has fallen toward international levels.

3.75 percent and 7.5 percent of gross assets would also be normal. The requirement of 2 percent of gross assets as a minimum tax payment thus does not appear excessive.

Some issues arise in instituting an assets tax. Should it be restricted to fixed assets or extended to include inventories and financial assets? Should deductions be allowed for debt liabilities incurred in connection with the fixed assets of the firm or for debt liabilities incurred more generally? How should the holdings by one firm of equities in another be treated? Rather than attempt to answer these questions directly, it might be useful to offer instead a sketch of some of the considerations involved.

First, a straight tax based on fixed assets, with no deductions for debt, would in effect eliminate the bias toward debt financing that is implicit in the income taxation of firms in most countries.[48] Second, it appears excessive to allow a firm's total debt to be offset against only its fixed assets; any offset offered should be limited to debt incurred in connection with fixed assets. Third, extending this tax to cover all assets and allowing the offset of all debt would end up covering only net worth, thereby introducing a whole host of complications that are absent when fixed assets alone are involved.[49] On the whole, and recognizing the use of this tax as a minimum tax, there is much to be said for restricting it to fixed assets and not allowing any offset for debt. Fourth, although firms with losses on their books will always complain about this minimum tax, the difficulties involved in distinguishing between firms with genuine losses and those whose losses are the result of evasion suggest that, at most, leniency could be shown to firms with losses on their books by granting them a limited carry forward and postponement of their tax liability. A tougher stance would insist not only on losses on the books but also a negative cash flow as conditions of eligibility for such a carry forward.

The Value-Added Tax

Exempted Sectors

Colombia has made huge advances in designing and administering the VAT during the 1990s. From a shaky structure built on excessively naive and hope-

ful premises, it has evolved into a robust and sturdy modern tax with a high revenue yield potential that is well adapted to administrative exigencies.

An important achievement in the recent reform of the VAT is the virtual elimination of the zero-rated category, including through the transfer of many items from this category to the exempted category, which is outside the VAT system. In this connection, it should first be emphasized that excluding an activity from the VAT system does not necessarily mean that revenue is lost. Revenue is lost only to the degree that an exempted entity sells to purchasers (such as individual households) who are themselves outside the system. To the degree that an entity sells to firms that are inside the system, these firms effectively pay for both their own value added and for the full cost of the product that they buy from the exempted entity.

Second, when an exempted entity buys from sellers who are within the VAT network, it naturally pays the tax that is built into the prices of the products that it buys. As the entity does not belong to the VAT network, it is not eligible to claim the credits that could otherwise be used to offset the tax. Taxes collected in this way represent extra revenue that is received as a consequence of excluding activities from the network.

It must be added that decisions made to exclude an activity or sector from the VAT network are not generally taken with the intention of collecting more revenue from that sector by failing to give credit for the tax paid on inputs. Rather, the failure to give credit for such taxes is a simple but not particularly desired consequence of leaving an activity out of the VAT system. Zero rating an activity will ensure that it gets credit for the VAT embodied in its inputs, but, for all its conceptual elegance, the practice of zero rating creates a number of administrative problems and significantly increases evasion. In this context, the shifting of many activities from the zero-rated to the exempted category in Colombia should be considered as attempts to improve the effectiveness of tax administration.

Exemption of Selected Imports

The above discussion is a prelude to a discussion of the cases in which certain imported goods are, in effect, kept zero rated by not only exempting the final good but also its inputs. The best way to understand the treatment of these goods is in terms of the agricultural sector, which is now almost entirely exempted from the VAT network. This situation automatically implies that the agricultural sector will fail to receive credit for certain types of inputs—for example, lumber, paints, automobiles, trucks, hand tools, and other hardware. Certainly, it makes sense

---

[48]As private portfolios increasingly include foreign assets, the bias toward debt financing is further reduced through the assets tax.

[49]Not surprisingly, Colombia's minimum income tax contribution based on net worth was never a significant revenue producer. Also, the base of the tax has been reduced sequentially from 6 percent of net worth in 1992 to 5 percent of net worth in 1993 and to 4 percent of net worth in 1994 and thereafter.

to exempt those inputs that are more or less exclusively destined for agricultural uses, and which are mainly imported, such as agricultural tractors and other farm machinery. As these items are not being produced in Colombia and are unlikely to be produced domestically in the near future, it seems quite unnecessary to charge a tax at the border that will become a permanent part of the price structure of goods in the exempted category. Not taxing these items is therefore a way of palliating a not particularly desired effect of a policy whose main rationale (other than in the agricultural sector) is administrative in nature.

The above line of reasoning is persuasive, but it can easily lead to a proliferation of VAT exemptions for imports, which, in turn, could undo the robustness and administrative simplicity of the present system. These exemptions should be carefully scrutinized to ensure that they are a help rather than a hindrance to the authorities.

Put another way, the cleanest solution in the long run would be to convert the VAT into a purely consumption-type tax on all purchases. Capital goods, raw materials, and intermediate products purchases could then be credited against the sale of finished products (except for agricultural products and clearly identifiable inputs of the agricultural sector, which, for reasons of administration, could remain exempted). There should be no difference in the treatment of sources or the use of inputs (or outputs) under the VAT.

Colombia's VAT has come a long way toward reaching this norm through the passage of Law No. 6 of 1992. Nevertheless, the differential treatment for VAT purposes of capital goods continues. Imported capital goods used in basic industries are exempted; meanwhile, the VAT paid on other capital goods is creditable against the income tax (effectively, within a limit). Thus, while the system contains the essential elements of a consumption-type VAT, it could be hampered by possible bureaucratic intervention in the definition of capital goods and listing of basic industries, as well as by administrative difficulties. Furthermore, the current system does not eliminate the economic distortions that result from cascading. Hence, a complete conversion to a consumption-type VAT—including a full credit mechanism within the VAT structure—should be undertaken at an appropriate time in the future.

Elimination of Special VAT Rates

With the reforms that have been made, Colombia's VAT system has been strengthened considerably. Nevertheless, one element that tends to compromise its coherency is the existence of special rates other than the general rate, which is now 14 percent. For-tunately, these special rates apply to only a few items: beer carries a rate of 8 percent; insurance contracted abroad is charged a 15 percent rate; certain vehicles and motorcycles carry a 20 percent rate; wine, liquor, and luxury cars up to US$35,000 in price are charged 35 percent; and luxury cars over US$35,000 carry a 45 percent rate.

There seems to be little problem involved in incorporating beer and foreign insurance contracts into the general rate of 14 percent. The items with higher rates are a different matter, as these rates appear to be dictated by special motives. All of them could be incorporated into the general rate of the VAT, with excise taxes set up in conjunction with the VAT to deal with the categories that now carry rates of 20 percent, 35 percent, and 45 percent. The administrative effort needed to collect these moneys under an excise tax label should be significantly less than the effort now required to deal with them under a VAT label. There should also be a significant reduction in compliance costs, because entities such as automobile dealerships, which now keep a separate accounting of vehicles entering under different rates, could apply a single rate under a unified VAT. Moreover, if the excises were levied at the importation or manufacturing stage in Colombia, businesses would not have to consider excise taxes at all (as they would simply be part of the prices paid for vehicles).[50]

The Future of the General Rate of the VAT

With a robust and highly viable VAT, Colombia can look forward to a future characterized by fiscal prudence and responsibility. In the present decade, there is a well-justified emphasis on downsizing government and exercising greater control of public expenditures, which should lead to a lowering of the level of taxation required for budgetary responsibility. However, keeping the budget reasonably well balanced is a priority that must prevail, regardless of the level of government outlays. Moreover, in contemplating the needs of Colombia in such fields as health, education, sanitation, and road building, it is difficult to see how cutting unneeded items out of the present budget could in the end lead to a lower total outlay.

It should be noted that higher VAT rates are in place and are being administered with reasonable success in countries such as Argentina (18 percent), Bolivia (15 percent), Brazil (17 percent), Chile (18 percent), Peru (18 percent), and Uruguay (22 percent). A higher VAT rate in itself has no virtue; rather, such an increase is one of the significant op-

---

[50]If excises were assigned to lower levels of government, revenue sources other than a multiple-rated VAT might be sought at the federal level.

tions available for consideration in the context of the overall level of government expenditures, the rates and revenue yields of other taxes, and the evolution of revenue-sharing and tax assignment rules (see Wiesner, 1992).

Indexing the Tax System for Business Firms

Indexation of the tax system has been one of the true triumphs of fiscal reform in Colombia in recent years. Moreover, there is no country in the world—including Canada, France, Germany, Korea, Malaysia, and the United States, not to mention China or the newly independent states of the former Soviet Union—whose overall fiscal and economic policies could not benefit greatly from implementing the type of indexation that has been introduced in Colombia. The reasons given for not introducing indexing in other countries are very weak indeed. In the main, governments fear that if they sponsor indexing legislation, they will be accused of planning on inflation or at least of having only a weak resolve to combat it. Hence, most governments have not indexed their tax systems.

The best time for a country to institute indexing is when inflation is low, as it inoculates the country forever against some of the worst consequences of inflation at essentially no cost. Certainly, as far as business income is concerned, only benefits—and no costs—are involved in indexing a country's tax system.

One of the most troublesome problems related to introducing indexed tax systems has been the resistance of certain sectors and groups to the use of a single index as a measure of inflation. Yet, it is only by using a single index that the logical simplicity and clarity of an indexing system can be revealed. In establishing an indexed tax system, therefore, an important distinction is to be made between movements of the general price level (inflation) and movements of relative prices of goods, services, and assets of different types.

All too often, pressures arise to use sector-specific or even commodity-specific indexes of prices to adjust for inflation. At the extreme, this idea could take the form of replacement cost accounting, which separately adjusts for inflation each commodity that is held in inventory by a firm. Colombia did not fall prey to this temptation in setting up its system of indexation. However, there appears to be a weakness in Colombia's treatment of inventories under this system, stemming from the use of quarterly adjustments of prices and the arbitrary assignment to each quarter of precisely one fourth of the year's inflation. It should not be difficult for the authorities to allow

the indexing system to reflect each quarter's actual rate of inflation, or even to adopt a system of monthly indexation that is applicable to both inventories and fixed assets.

For example, under the Colombian system, a fixed asset bought in May is assigned an inflationary write-up for the year on the basis of the rate at which the general price level rose between May and December. Similarly, an asset bought in October would receive a write-up based on the rise of prices from October to December. Meanwhile, an asset sold in August would receive a write-up (from its December value of the previous year) corresponding to the inflation rate between December and August. The firm would then declare a capital gain or loss based on the difference between the written-up value of the asset and the actual price at which it was sold.

There seems to be no cogent reason why this treatment of fixed assets could not be applied by the authorities to all inventory items. Basically, each inventory item could be written up on the basis of the rate of inflation occurring between the month of purchase and the month of sale, resulting in a capital gain or loss equal to the difference between the written-up price and the actual sale price.

There would be no need to track each item laboriously and adjust its value every month. Rather, the total stack of inventories could be adjusted monthly. Each month, the stock would be augmented by the inflationary adjustment, plus purchases during the month (at actual purchase prices), minus sales during the month (at actual prices when purchased, augmented by the percentage increment of the index between the month of purchase and the month of sale). Determination of capital gains or losses would thus be kept separate from the actual inventory accounting.

Moreover, the system described above is completely applicable, regardless of whether "first in, first out" or "last in, first out" accounting procedures are used. Either way, no serious problems, either with respect to accounting by the firm or administration by the tax authorities, are entailed.

The Colombian indexing system deviates from the principle of using a single index of inflation in one respect: its treatment of assets denominated in foreign currency. The Colombian system permits assets and debts expressed in U.S. dollars, deutsche mark, and yen to be adjusted by the Colombian peso price of the respective currencies. A purist in the theory and application of indexing could appropriately object to this treatment; however, maintaining this treatment of foreign currency can be justified on the grounds that the business firms most involved in foreign currency operations have a strong desire to keep it that way. Otherwise, it would be better to treat foreign currency assets (or at least the assets denominated in the major currencies), in the same way as real assets are treated.

Contracts that are indexed by a numeraire different from the one used by the tax authorities could also be standardized. The contracts could be written up on the basis of the tax authority's index during each accounting period, and the increment assigned as a profit or loss depending on whether the write-up applied to an asset or liability. Then, upon final liquidation, the capital gain or loss could be indexed on the basis of the difference between the final settlement price and the accounting value that resulted from the standard index adjustment. As a matter of priority, standardizing the treatment of indexed contracts as simple real assets or liabilities should take precedence over applying standard indexing procedures to assets and liabilities expressed in the world's major currencies.

Tax Incentives

There are many different types of tax incentives that can be employed. Strangely, the three incentives that are most widely used—tax credits to gross investment, tax holidays, and percentage depletion and related treatments for oil exploration—tend to be the most objectionable from an economic point of view. A fourth kind of tax incentive—accelerated depreciation—is very difficult to classify or rate because, inter alia, depreciation can take so many forms, its rate of acceleration can vary considerably, and it can sometimes change the general shape of the depreciation profile drastically. On the whole, however, one can say that accelerated depreciation schemes have been far less costly in terms of economic inefficiency and false incentives than the other types of tax incentives mentioned.

A rather cursory examination of the existing treatments makes it obvious that Colombia has demonstrated wisdom and restraint in the field of tax incentives. Colombia's existing tax system embodies some tax incentives to investment, but not the types of incentives with the most severe consequences. The tax incentive most employed is accelerated depreciation, the least objectionable of the four.

However, the Colombian authorities could establish a more generalized scheme of accelerated depreciation that would compare favorably with the depreciation schemes applied most frequently in other countries. The scheme proposed is very simple: allow a certain fraction of an asset's cost to be expensed in its year of acquisition and insist that the remainder be depreciated in the standard fashion over the normal economic life of the asset. Thus, if a particular asset followed a normal straight-line depreciation pattern over ten years, its value would de-

scribe a trajectory of 100 percent, 90 percent, 80 percent, and so on, until reaching zero percent. A weak incentive given to this asset would lead to a book value trajectory along the lines of 100 percent, 80 percent, 72 percent, 64 percent, and so on, until zero percent was reached. A sharper incentive would give it a trajectory of 100 percent, 50 percent, 45 percent, 40 percent, and so on. If the normal depreciation pattern were exponential at 20 percent, the book value would drop from 100 percent to 80 percent to 64 percent, and so on. In this case, a strong incentive would shift this trajectory to 100 percent, 50 percent, 40 percent, 32 percent, and so on, until zero percent was reached.

It is clear that this scheme accelerates depreciation in every case, thus giving a tax incentive to investment. The great virtue of this method is that it produces no anomalous results. For example, it does not change the economic ordering of projects, such as by giving enterprises private incentives to undertake projects with prospective economic yields of, say, 6 percent while rejecting under the same incentive scheme other projects with prospective economic yields of, say, 11 percent.

The incentive scheme described above is fully calibrated. If the normal operations of the capital market lead companies to accept investments with gross-of-tax prospective yields of greater than 20 percent and to reject those promising yields of less than 20 percent, a mild incentive—such as expensing one fourth of the asset cost in its first year—might lower the critical prospective yield from 20 percent to 18 percent, while a sharper incentive might reduce it to 16 percent or 15 percent.

Under this scheme, the extreme incentive that can be employed is full expensing. Of course, full expensing does not distort choices among the assets subject to it; in effect, it amounts to annulling the tax on enterprise income, not by actually eliminating the tax but by making the government a "t percent" partner in the business. Through the expensing of the investment as well as of all current outlays, the government effectively pays t percent of all costs. However, after deducting these expenses, the government then collects t percent of any remaining surpluses and, hence, shares t percent in the tax fruits of any investments or endeavors. There are several administrative and harmonization issues, however, associated with this type of cash-flow tax. (For a detailed discussion, see Shome and Schutte (1993)).

Partial expensing at the fraction α means that the government becomes an αt percent partner in the enterprise, rather than simply a t percent partner. The government remains a taxing agent for the remaining $(1 - \alpha)$ percent of the costs and benefits of the investment.

Conclusion

Colombian tax policy changes in the 1990s have not only continued the decades-long tradition of incremental tax reform but have also hastened the rationalization of tax policy by reducing distortions, improving equity, and simplifying the overall structure. The income tax rate structure was scaled back, personal and corporate income taxes were integrated, and inflation indexing was introduced. Furthermore, the VAT closely approached a consumption-type structure, and customs tariffs underwent fundamental reform.

The direction of tax reform in Colombia points toward the adoption of a uniform tariff and a purely consumption-type VAT with a uniform rate, as well as the correction of the remaining few anomalies in the income tax structure. Also, with the simplification of the overall tax structure, it remains for the revenue-sharing and tax assignment rules to be rationalized in line with the devolvement of expenditure responsibilities to lower levels of government. To conclude, it is clear that although selected improvements are still needed, those made thus far in the 1990s have been quite impressive.

Appendix I   Summary of Tax System as of June 30, 1994

Tax	Nature of Tax	Exemptions and Deductions	Rates

I. Taxes on Net Income and Profits

Taxes on Business Enterprise Income (Impuesto a la Renta)
Decrees No. 1979, 2053, 2217, 2310, and 2348 of 1974; Laws No. 18 of 1969, 49 of 1975, 20 of 1979, 9 of 1983, 75 of 1986, and 49 of 1990; Decree No. 1744 of 1991; and Laws No. 6 of 1992 and 98 of 1993. All these rules are compiled in the Colombian tax statutes (Decree No. 624 of 1989).

Applies in principle to all corporations, including stock companies, limited companies, and partnerships. The tax is levied on overall net profits of Colombian enterprises (including most state or industrial) and on all Colombian-source income of foreign enterprises. Net profit is presumed to be not less than 5 percent of the firm's net worth for 1993, and 4 percent for subsequent years. All values of income, outlays, and main balance sheet accounts are subject to full adjustment beginning in 1992. The tax legislation allows for inflation effects on profits and losses.

Interest income from certain government bonds is exempt. Double taxation is eliminated when corporations pay taxes on income, so that dividends are tax free. Various tax credits are granted, including for dividends obtained by corporations, charitable contributions, and foreign taxes paid. Exemptions are granted for community enterprises, as well as enterprises located in free zones and editorial businesses. Also exempt are exploration ventures involving hydrocarbons and mines for up to 10 percent of the gross value of investment in explorations, and in stock funds and livestock corporation funds. Net profits of enterprises that were established in the Nevado del Ruiz zone prior to 1988 are partially exempt. Repatriated profits and dividends from foreign investments are exempt from a surtax on remittances if reinvested for five years.

The rate for all corporations is 30 percent, plus a surtax of 7.5 percent, put into effect during 1993–97. Taxpayers not required to submit tax declarations are exempt from the surtax. There is a surtax of 12 percent on profits and income remittances of existing foreign non-oil investments (the rate will be reduced gradually to 7 percent by 1996) and 15 percent on existing foreign oil investment for 1993–95 (which will become 12 percent starting in 1996). The rate on all other new foreign investments is 12 percent, starting in 1993.

Personal Income Tax (Impuesto a la Renta)
Law No. 18 of 1969; Decrees No. 2053 and 2347 of 1975, 20 of 1979, 9 of 1983, 55 of 1985, and 75 of 1986; Decrees No. 3715 and 3750 of 1986 and 2503 of 1987; Law No. 49 of 1990 and Decree No. 1653 of 1991; and Laws No. 6 of 1992, 98 of 1993, and 100 of 1993. All these rules are compiled in the Colombian tax statutes (Decree No. 624 of 1989).

Levied on overall income of Colombian residents and on all Colombian-source income of residents. Taxes on wage income, interest, and dividends are withheld at source. Taxpayers with at least 80 percent of their income subject to withholding at source, overall income of up to Col$25.6 million a year, and wealth of up to Col$49.2 million are not required to make tax declarations. Net income is presumed to be not less than 5 percent of the value of net wealth for 1993 and 4 percent starting in 1994, unless a lower income can be proved owing to forces outside the individual's control (for example, flooding or drought). Nonmonetary assets expressed in domestic currency, as well as the value of fixed assets, are subject to full yearly adjustments for inflation.

Various types of income are exempt, including sickness and maternity benefits and burial benefits, as well as compensation for vacations, job-related accidents, unemployment, and representation outlays by government officials. Also exempt are pensions, basic wages of army and police forces, interest received on government securities (issued before September 30, 1974), and dividends for Colombian residents. Other deductions include mortgage interest payments and contributions to pension funds by employees and employers. Through Law No. 98 of 1993, wide exemptions are granted for editing, printing, and marketing books and printed materials, including copyrights and royalties.

For fiscal year 1993, marginal rates ranged from zero percent on taxable income of less than Col$5 million to 30 percent on taxable income in excess of Col$24.8 million. A surtax of 25 percent will be in effect during 1993–97. Taxpayers not required to submit tax declarations are exempt from the surtax.

Tax System *(continued)*

Tax	Nature of Tax	Exemptions and Deductions	Rates
Tax on Windfall Income (Ganancias Ocasionales) Decrees No. 2053 and 2274 of 1974; Law No. 20 of 1979; Decrees No. 3211 of 1979, 727 of 1980, and 2655 of 1981; and Laws No. 75 of 1986, 49 of 1990, and 6 of 1992.	Levied on net capital gains arising from the sale of assets held for at least two years and on payments to shareholders beyond earned capital that have operated for at least two years. Also levied on assets, losses, and profits on income acquired through inheritances, bequests, or gifts (net of inheritances and gift taxes), and prizes obtained in, inter alia, open contests, lotteries, and raffles.	Capital gains arising from the sale of stocks are exempt. In the case of inheritances, the first Col$5 million for the surviving spouse and immediate family are exempt, as well as 20 percent with a limit of Col$5 million for other survivors. Contributions to the Nevado del Ruiz Reconstruction Fund (RESURGIR) and for the Causa Natural Disaster Fund are also exempt.	For corporations, the rate is 39 percent for Colombian residents in accordance with personal income tax rates. For nonresidents, a 30 percent windfall rate applies to income from prizes, with a 20 percent rate applied to income from lotteries or bets.

II. Social Security Contributions

Tax	Nature of Tax	Exemptions and Deductions	Rates
Law No. 100 of 1993; and Decrees No. 047, 048, 530, 692, 695, 656, 720, 721, 682, 740, 773, 813, 807, and 903 of 1994.	Levied on employers and employees as a percentage of the wage bill, in order to finance health programs, disability and life insurance, and future pension plans. The new social security system, including the establishment of a system based on individual capitalization accounts, has been applied since April 1, 1994.	None.	In 1994, social security contributions accounted for 23.5 percent of the wage bill. Tax rates for employers' contributions to two insurance funds—pension disability or death, and maternity and general sickness—were 8.625 percent and 8 percent of the wage bill, respectively, for a total of 16.625 percent. Tax rates for employees' contributions to those two funds were 2.875 percent and 4 percent of the wage bill, respectively, for a total of 6.875 percent. Contributions to the two funds thus amounted to 11.5 percent and 12 percent, respectively, of the wage bill in 1994. Tax rates for pension plan disability or death will increase to 12.5 percent in 1995 and 13.5 percent in 1996.

III. Payroll Taxes

Tax	Nature of Tax	Exemptions and Deductions	Rates
Colombian Institute for Family Welfare (Instituto Colombiano de Bienestar Familiar (ICBF)) Laws No. 75 of 1968, 27 of 1974, and 89 of 1988; and Decree No. 626 of 1975.	Proceeds are earmarked for education and nutrition programs for employees' children aged up to 7 years.	Not applicable to certain public sector establishments.	The rate is 3 percent of the monthly payroll.
National Services for Apprenticeship (Servicio Nacional de Aprendizaje (SENA)) Law No. 58 of 1963; Decree No. 3128 of 1968; Law No. 21 of 1982; and Decree No. 27 of 1990.	Proceeds are earmarked, in part, to provide on-the-job and apprenticeship training.	Firms with up to ten workers or with capital of less than Col$50,000 are exempt.	The rate is 2 percent of the monthly payroll.

Tax System *(continued)*

Tax	Nature of Tax	Exemptions and Deductions	Rates
Family Benefit Section (Cajas de Compensación Familiar) Law No. 58 of 1963; Decree No. 3123 of 1968; Law No. 21 of 1982; and Decree No. 27 of 1990.	Proceeds are earmarked as a family subsidy to be distributed to the employees of the taxpayer in proportion to the number of the employees' children. The proceeds also provide groceries to the employees.	Firms with no more than ten workers or with capital of less than Col$30,000.	The rate is 4 percent of the monthly payroll.

IV. Property Taxes

Tax	Nature of Tax	Exemptions and Deductions	Rates
Net Wealth Tax (Impuesto al Patrimonio) Law No. 49 of 1990.	The net wealth tax was eliminated in 1992.	None.	None.

V. Taxes on Goods and Services

Tax	Nature of Tax	Exemptions and Deductions	Rates
Value-Added Tax (Impuesta a las Ventas) Law No. 21 of 1963; Decrees No. 1988, 2368, 2810, and 2803 of 1974; Decrees No. 1980, 232, and 3541 of 1983; and Laws No. 12 of 1986, 49 of 1990, 6 of 1992, and 98 of 1993. All these rules are compiled in the Colombian tax statutes (Decree No. 624 of 1989).	Operated in general as a value-added tax of the consumption type (firms are granted tax credit for value-added tax payments on raw materials). Includes many goods and services.	Exemptions are granted to foodstuffs and other basic goods; exports; agricultural imports; agro-industry products; pharmaceuticals; cultural and scientific books; antiques and arts; imports of higher-education institutions; domestic transportation; medical and educational services; advertising; leasing; the repair of marine vessels and foreign aircraft; and the communities of San Andres and Providencia.	The general rate is 14 percent for 1993–97 and 12 percent thereafter. Other rates are 8 percent on domestic beer; 15 percent on insurance contracted abroad; 20 percent on certain vehicles and motorcycles; 35 percent on wine, liquor, luxury cars valued up to US$35,000, and recreational boats; and 45 percent on private aircraft and luxury cars valued over US$35,000.
Tax on Petroleum Products Laws No. 64 of 1967, 30 of 1982, and 55 of 1985; Decrees No. 1013 of 1982 and 1222 of 1986; and Law No. 6 of 1992.	Levied on the sale price of gasoline and petroleum derivatives. Since 1993, departments and municipalities have been receiving an amount equal to 18 percent of the difference between the current final price of gasoline and its level in July 1992. The state-owned oil company, ECOPETROL, effectively bears the burden of this scheme.	Marine fuel and derived lubricants are exempt, as are certain derivatives consumed by electricity plants in a number of departments; in a few municipalities, consumption is exempt.	A rate of 24.8 percent applies to petroleum products, and 23.4 percent to the consumer price of gasoline and diesel.
Surtax on Mining Production Law No. 6 of 1992.	Levied on the production of crude oil, natural gas, coal, and nickel during 1993–97.	None.	Light crude Col$900/bbl. Heavy crude Col$500/bbl. Natural gas Col$0.03/cu.ft. Coal Col$200/ton Nickel Col$31/lb.
Excise Taxes Decree No. 1222 of 1986; Law No. 10 of 1990; and Decree No. 1280 of 1994.	Imposed on beer, liquor, tobacco products, international travel tickets, coal, and the distribution of gasoline.	None.	A 40 percent tax is placed on beer and liquor; 45 percent on domestic cigarettes and tobacco; and 45 percent on imported cigarettes.

Tax System *(concluded)*

Tax	Nature of Tax	Exemptions and Deductions	Rates

VI. Taxes on International Trade

Taxes on Imports

Decree No. 2374 of 1974; Laws No. 50 of 1984, 75 of 1986, 84 of 1988, and 49 of 1990; Law No. 7 of 1971; and Decrees No. 2666 of 1984, 971 of 1993, 3104 of 1990, and 1909 of 1992.

Import tariffs are levied on the c.i.f. value of most products imported into Colombia.

Certain public and all military agencies are exempt. Other exemptions include those granted to industrial duty-free zones; enterprises benefiting from duty drawbacks under the Vallejo Plan; and regional trade accords such as the Andean Pact.

A rate of 5 percent is levied on imported raw materials and capital equipment, liquor, cigarettes, and domestic appliances; 15 percent on most domestically produced capital equipment and pharmaceuticals; and 20 percent on consumption goods. Most agricultural goods are taxed at a fixed rate of 15 percent, plus a variable rate aimed at keeping import prices within a specified band. A 35 percent rate is applied to luxury goods (for example, expensive automobiles).

Taxes on Exports

Decrees No. 444 of 1967, 2374 of 1974, and 2835 of 1986; and Laws No. 9 of 1991 and 7 of 1971.

Exports of coffee are subject to an ad valorem tax based on the surrender price, which is collected at the time of foreign exchange receipt.

None.

The export tax rate is 6.4 percent, of which 3.7 percent is earmarked for the National Coffee Federation and 2.7 percent for the National Coffee Fund.

VII. Stamp Taxes (Timbre)

Laws No. 2 of 1976 and 39 of 1981; Decrees No. 3212 of 1979 and 450 of 1981; Law No. 75 of 1986 and Decree No. 3749 of 1986; and Law No. 6 of 1992. All these rules are compiled in the Colombian tax statutes (Decree No. 624 of 1989).

Levied on many official and commercial documents with contents obligations of more than Col$20 million. Stamp taxes are levied also on airport departures for abroad; on the commercial value of privately owned vehicles; and on airport loading.

Exemptions are granted to all public agencies and charitable organizations. Receipts and certain commercial documents are also exempt.

The general rate is 0.5 percent on document value. Tariffs vary, depending on the document: rates range from 0.8 percent to 2.5 percent on the commercial value of vehicles.

Appendix II   Potential VAT Collections from the Input-Output Matrix and Taxpayer Declarations

In this appendix, Tables 20–22 demonstrate the impact of alternative structural configurations of the value-added tax (VAT), using the 1988 input-output matrix. These data are compared with the results obtained from information in tax declarations on the taxable and creditable base (Table 23). Finally, the actual revenue loss from converting the VAT to a consumption-type tax (through Law No. 6 of 1992) is analyzed (Table 24).

As shown in Table 23, the potential tax base was calculated, using the input-output matrix and taking into account the VAT law (column 1 of Table 23). This calculation yielded a figure for potential gross VAT (column 3). However, examination of the codes used on the VAT declaration forms shows that only a portion of the gross output of each sector is taxed. Overall, approximately one third of gross output escapes taxation (column 4), including the effect of exports. When this ratio was applied to the gross potential VAT derived from the input-output matrix exercise, an estimate for "calculated" gross VAT, taking into account the effect of the declarations, was obtained (column 5).

It is clear from this exercise that the taxable base indicated by the declarations is much lower than the theoretical base derived from the input-output matrix. From "gross income" (line 1:BA on the VAT declaration form), the VAT form excludes all income from the exempted sectors, as well as exports, to arrive at "taxed income" (line 4:BD on the form). As exports account for less than one tenth of gross collections, the other exemptions and zero ratings must explain the remainder.

The same exercise can be carried out in terms of VAT credit for intermediate consumption. The amount of such credit calculated by the input-output matrix is shown in column 7 of Table 23. However, new estimates of VAT credit can be obtained (column 9) by applying the ratio of the gross VAT credited in taxpayers' declarations to gross VAT (column 8) to the estimated potential gross VAT (column 3). A comparison of column 7 and column 9 shows once again that VAT credit from the declarations is much greater than the theoretical credit determined from the input-output matrix. Accordingly, this is another area where there is a gap between potential collections and the amounts calculated from the declarations.

Table 20. Potential VAT Collections Prior to Passage of Law No. 49

(Base year = 1988; in billions of Colombian pesos, unless otherwise specified)

	Gross Output (1)	Effective VAT Rate (In percent) (2)[1]	Estimated Potential Gross VAT (3)	Intermediate Consumption (4)	VAT Credit for Intermediate Consumption (5)[2]	Imports (6)	Effective VAT Rate on Imports (In percent) (7)[3]	Potential VAT on Imports (8)	Exports (9)	VAT Credit for Exports (10)[4]	Estimated Net Potential VAT (11)[5]
Total	9,083.6	6.8	618.3	4,080.2	200.0	1,461.9	10.5	154.1	1,002.4	51.0	521.3
Mining	896.6	—	—	194.5	−13.5	18.1	—	—	505.3	7.6	5.9
Beverages	285.2	14.8	42.3	198.3	6.7	15.8	30.0	4.7	1.0	0.1	40.2
Tobacco	26.7	10.0	2.7	17.1	0.8	0.2	10.2	0.0	0.5	—	1.9
Textiles	643.8	10.0	64.4	371.4	24.7	52.9	10.0	5.3	139.6	14.0	31.0
Wood and furniture	110.8	10.0	11.1	57.3	3.3	2.4	10.0	0.2	3.7	0.4	7.7
Paper and printing	379.0	10.0	37.9	241.4	15.6	63.2	10.0	6.3	33.8	3.4	25.2
Chemicals, rubber, and plastic	967.8	7.5	72.9	725.1	57.8	486.2	7.5	36.6	74.7	5.6	46.2
Petroleum products	384.8	9.8	37.7	300.5	3.1	83.2	9.8	8.1	96.9	9.5	33.2
Processed mineral and nonmetallic goods	291.8	11.3	33.1	148.2	8.3	20.5	11.3	2.3	16.1	1.8	25.3
Processed metal goods	390.6	10.0	39.1	254.4	19.2	205.1	10.0	20.5	14.2	1.4	39.0
Machinery and equipment[6]	271.5	9.8	26.6	164.1	12.1	164.9	10.0	16.5	19.7	1.9	29.0
Transport equipment	255.3	18.9	48.1	170.5	13.8	249.2	18.9	47.0	1.9	0.4	81.0
Miscellaneous manufactures	77.9	11.3	8.8	36.2	3.0	43.2	11.3	4.9	7.5	0.8	9.8
Electricity, gas, and water[7]	381.8	1.4	5.2	35.9	2.2	—	—	—	—	—	2.9
Banks, insurance, and services[8]	952.1	2.8	27.1	220.2	2.2	31.1	—	—	21.8	0.6	24.3
Communications (telephone)	201.4	6.0	12.1	64.9	3.0	22.4	6.0	1.3	44.0	2.6	7.8
Personal services[9]	1,345.4	3.5	46.5	419.2	5.1	3.4	3.4	0.1	21.8	0.8	40.7
Retail trade	1,221.1	8.4[10]	102.9	461.0	32.7	—	—	—	—	—	70.2

Sources: Tax Studies Subdirectorate, Directorate of National Taxes; and IMF staff estimates.

[1] Average of the rate for each range (code) of the sectors. Column 3 is therefore not necessarily equal to the product of column 1 and column 2.

[2] Using the input-output matrix of 1988, the specific rate for each of the sector's inputs has been applied to the amount of that input; the total for all is reflected in this column.

[3] If the specific code is obvious, the relevant rate is applied. If not, the effective rate for gross output (column 2) is used.

[4] The effective rate for gross output (column 2) has been applied to the value of exports (column 9), except in the case of exempted goods, for which VAT credit for output is extended only if the goods are exported.

[5] (11) = (3) − (5) + (8) − (10).

[6] It is assumed that this import value is 40 percent of total imports, as the remaining 60 percent is not taxed.

[7] Gas only (output valued at Col$129.071 billion) is included in the base, at a rate of 4 percent.

[8] Insurance only (excluding life insurance) is included in the base (valued at Col$180.8 billion), at a rate of 15 percent.

[9] Two thirds (66 percent) of output was not taxed.

[10] This average has been determined on the basis of commercial markups for all sectors.

Table 21. Potential VAT Collections After Passage of Law No. 49
(Base year = 1988; in billions of Colombian pesos, unless otherwise specified)

	Gross Output (1)	Effective VAT Rate (In percent) (2)[1]	Estimated Potential Gross VAT (3)	Intermediate Consumption (4)	VAT Credit for Intermediate Consumption (5)[2]	Imports (6)	Effective VAT Rate on Imports (In percent) (7)[3]	Potential VAT on Imports (8)	Exports (9)	VAT Credit for Exports (10)[4]	Estimated Net Potential VAT (11)[5]
Total	11,333.2	6.6	748.7	5,735.5	187.6	1,542.8	11.4	176.0	1,584.2	66.1	671.0
Agricultural products[6]	2,249.6	—	—	1,604.8	-12.4	80.9	—	—	581.8	1.4	11.0
Mining	896.6	—	—	197.2	-16.2	18.1	—	—	505.3	9.1	7.1
Beverages	285.2	16.4	46.9	198.3	8.0	15.8	30.0	4.7	1.0	0.2	43.4
Tobacco	26.7	12.0	3.2	17.1	0.9	0.2	12.2	—	0.5	0.1	2.2
Textiles	643.8	12.0	77.3	371.4	29.6	52.9	12.0	6.4	139.6	16.8	37.2
Wood and furniture	110.8	12.0	13.3	57.3	3.9	2.4	12.0	0.3	3.7	0.4	9.2
Paper and printing	379.0	12.0	45.5	241.4	18.7	63.2	12.0	7.6	33.8	4.1	30.3
Chemicals, rubber, and plastic[6]	967.8	9.0	87.5	745.5	28.6	486.2	9.0	44.0	74.7	8.3	94.5
Petroleum products	384.8	12.0	46.2	300.5	3.7	83.2	12.0	10.0	96.9	11.6	40.8
Processed mineral and nonmetallic goods	291.8	12.0	35.0	148.2	9.9	20.5	12.0	2.5	16.1	1.9	25.6
Processed metal goods	390.6	12.0	46.9	254.4	23.0	205.1	12.0	24.6	14.2	1.7	46.8
Machinery and equipment[7]	271.5	11.7	31.9	164.1	14.5	164.9	12.0	19.8	19.7	2.3	34.9
Transport equipment	255.3	19.1	48.6	170.5	16.6	249.2	19.1	47.6	1.9	0.2	79.5
Miscellaneous manufactures	77.9	13.2	10.3	36.2	3.6	43.2	13.2	5.7	7.5	1.0	11.4
Electricity, gas, and water[8]	381.8	4.1	15.5	35.9	2.7	—	—	—	—	—	12.8
Banks, insurance, and services[9]	952.1	2.8	27.1	220.2	2.2	31.1	—	—	21.8	0.6	24.3
Communications (telephone)	201.4	12.0	24.2	64.9	3.6	22.4	12.0	2.7	44.0	5.3	17.9
Personal services[10]	1,345.4	4.9	66.3	446.7	7.2	3.4	4.9	0.2	21.8	1.1	58.2
Retail trade	1,221.1	10.1[11]	123.1	461.0	39.3	—	—	—	—	—	83.8

Sources: Tax Studies Subdirectorate, Directorate of National Taxes; and IMF staff estimates.

[1]Average of the rate for each range (code) of the sectors. Column 3 is therefore not necessarily equal to the product of column 1 and column 2.

[2]Using the input-output matrix of 1988, the specific rate for each of the sector's inputs has been applied to the amount of that input; the total for all is reflected in this column.

[3]If the specific code is obvious, the relevant rate is applied. If not, the effective rate for gross output (column 2) is used.

[4]The effective rate for gross output (column 2) has been applied to the value of exports (column 9), except in the case of exempted goods, for which VAT credit for output is extended only if the goods are exported.

[5](11) = (3) − (5) + (8) − (10).

[6]The effect of moving some products from the zero-rated list to the exempted list is incorporated in this exercise. It is obvious in drawing comparisons with the situation prior to Law No. 49 that the theoretical effect on collections should not be insignificant.

[7]It is assumed that this import value is 40 percent of total imports, as the remaining 60 percent is not taxed.

[8]Gas only (output valued at Col$129.071 billion) is included in the base, at a rate of 4 percent.

[9]Insurance only (excluding life insurance) is included in the base (valued at Col$180.8 billion), at a rate of 15 percent.

[10]The effect of including the new services in the base is incorporated.

[11]20 percent above the commercial margins prior to implementation of Law No. 49.

Table 22. Potential VAT Collections: An Alternative Structure

(Base year = 1988; in billions of Colombian pesos, unless otherwise specified)

	Gross Output (1)	Effective VAT Rate (In percent) (2)[1]	Estimated Potential Gross VAT (3)	Intermediate Consumption (4)	VAT Credit for Intermediate Consumption (5)[2]	Imports (6)	Effective VAT Rate on Imports (In percent) (7)[3]	Potential VAT on Imports (8)	Exports (9)	VAT Credit for Exports (10)[4]	Estimated Net Potential VAT (11)[5]
Total	12,763.6	7.9	1,005.7	6,375.1	288.6	1,707.7	8.9	151.8	1,603.9	117.0	751.9
Agricultural products[6]	2,249.6	—	—	1,604.8	-12.4	80.9	—	—	581.8	1.4	11.0
Mining[7]	896.6	12.0	107.6	181.0	16.2	18.1	12.0	2.2	505.3	60.6	32.9
Beverages	285.2	12.0	34.2	198.3	8.0	15.8	12.0	1.9	1.0	0.1	28.0
Tobacco	26.7	12.0	3.2	17.1	0.9	0.2	12.2	—	0.5	0.1	2.2
Textiles	643.8	12.0	77.3	371.4	29.6	52.9	12.0	6.4	139.6	16.8	37.2
Wood and furniture	110.8	12.0	13.3	57.3	3.9	2.4	12.0	0.3	3.7	0.4	9.2
Paper and printing	379.0	12.0	45.5	241.4	18.7	63.2	12.0	7.6	33.8	4.1	30.3
Chemicals, rubber, and plastic[6]	967.8	12.0	116.1	725.1	69.3	486.2	12.0	58.3	74.7	9.0	96.2
Petroleum products	384.8	12.0	46.2	300.5	3.7	83.2	12.0	10.0	96.9	11.6	40.8
Processed mineral and nonmetallic goods	291.8	12.0	35.0	148.2	9.9	20.5	12.0	2.5	16.1	1.9	25.6
Processed metal goods	390.6	12.0	46.9	254.4	23.0	205.1	12.0	24.6	14.2	1.7	46.8
Machinery and equipment	271.5	12.0	32.6	164.1	14.5	164.9	12.0	19.8	19.7	2.4	35.5
Effect of credit[8]	215.5	-12.0	-25.9	128.7	-11.4	164.9	-12.0	-19.8	19.7	-2.4	-31.9
Transport equipment	255.3	12.0	30.6	170.5	16.6	249.2	12.0	29.9	1.9	0.2	43.7
Miscellaneous manufactures	77.9	12.0	9.4	36.2	3.6	43.2	12.0	5.2	7.5	0.9	10.0
Electricity, gas, and water[9]	381.8	12.0	45.8	106.1	7.9	—	—	—	—	—	37.9
Banks, insurance, and services[10]	952.1	2.8	27.1	220.2	2.2	31.1	—	—	21.8	0.6	24.3
Communications (telephone)	215.0	12.0	25.8	64.9	3.6	22.4	12.0	2.7	44.0	5.3	19.6
Personal services[11]	1,345.4	10.3	138.6	446.7	15.1	3.4	10.3	0.3	21.8	2.2	121.7
Construction[12]	1,201.4	6.1	73.3	477.3	26.1	—	—	—	—	—	47.2
Retail trade	1,221.1	10.1	123.1	461.0	39.3	—	—	—	—	—	83.8

Sources: Tax Studies Subdirectorate, Directorate of National Taxes; and IMF staff estimates.

[1] Average of the rate for each range (code) of the sectors. Column 3 is therefore not necessarily equal to the product of column 1 and column 2.

[2] Using the input-output matrix of 1988, the specific rate for each of the sector's inputs has been applied to the amount of that input; the total for all is reflected in this column.

[3] If the specific code is obvious, the relevant rate is applied. If not, the effective rate for gross output (column 2) is used.

[4] The effective rate for gross output (column 2) has been applied to the value of exports (column 9), except in the case of exempted goods, for which VAT credit for output is extended only if the goods are exported.

[5] (11) = (3) − (5) + (8) − (10).

[6] The effect of moving some products from the zero-rated list to the exempted list is incorporated in this exercise. It is obvious in drawing comparisons with the situation prior to Law No. 49 that the theoretical effect on collections should not be insignificant.

[7] Taxed, while excluded under Law No. 49.

[8] Not including household appliances and comparable goods.

[9] Electricity and water are included in the VAT base.

[10] Insurance only (excluding life insurance) is included in the base (valued at Col\$180.8 billion), at a rate of 15 percent.

[11] Includes, apart from the services taxed under Law No. 49, additional services, such as legal, accounting, advertising, rental, security, technical expertise, and theaters and culture, as well as services provided by physicians, veterinary doctors, and hairdressers and beauty parlors.

[12] Civil works (Col\$590.778 billion) are not included in the base.

Table 23. Collections Calculated on the Basis of VAT Declarations Prior to Passage of Law No. 49

(Base year = 1988; in billions of Colombian pesos, unless otherwise specified)

	Gross Output (GO) (1)	Effective VAT Rate (In percent) (2)[1]	Estimated Potential Gross VAT (3)	Ratio of GO Covered in Declarations to GO (4)[2]	Estimated Calculated Gross VAT (5)[3]	Intermediate Consumption (6)	VAT Credit for Intermediate Consumption (7)[4]	Ratio of Gross VAT Credited in Declarations to Gross VAT (8)	Estimated Calculated VAT Credit (9)[5]	Imports (10)	Effective VAT Rate on Imports (In percent) (11)[6]	Potential VAT on Imports (12)	Estimated Calculated Net VAT (13)[7]
Total	9,083.6	6.8	618.3	0.699	432.2	4,080.2	200.0	0.616	384.0	1,461.9	10.5	154.1	202.3
Mining	896.6	—	—	0.066	—	194.5	−13.5	—	—	18.1	—	—	—
Beverages	285.2	14.8	42.3	0.425	18.0	198.3	6.7	0.630	26.6	15.8	30.0	4.7	−3.9
Tobacco	26.7	10.0	2.7	0.752	2.0	17.1	0.8	0.345	0.9	0.2	10.2	—	1.1
Textiles	643.8	10.0	64.4	0.838	54.0	371.4	24.7	0.623	40.1	52.9	10.0	5.3	19.1
Wood and furniture	10.8	10.0	11.1	0.790	8.7	57.3	3.3	0.468	5.2	2.4	10.0	0.2	3.8
Paper and printing	379.0	10.0	37.9	0.955	36.2	241.4	15.6	0.650	24.6	63.2	10.0	6.3	17.9
Chemicals, rubber, and plastic	967.8	7.5	72.9	0.580	42.3	725.1	57.8	0.788	57.5	486.2	7.5	36.6	21.5
Petroleum products	384.8	9.8	37.7	0.832	31.3	300.5	3.1	0.723	27.2	83.2	9.8	8.1	12.2
Processed mineral and nonmetallic goods	291.8	11.3	33.1	0.349	11.6	148.2	8.3	0.432	14.3	20.5	11.3	2.3	−0.4

	(1)	(2)	(3)	(4)	(5)	(6)	(7)	(8)	(9)	(10)	(11)	(12)	(13)
Processed metal goods	390.6	10.0	39.1	0.815	31.8	254.4	19.2	0.565	22.1	205.1	10.0	20.5	30.3
Machinery and equipment[8]	271.5	9.8	26.6	0.929	24.7	164.1	12.1	0.693	18.4	164.9	10.0	16.5	22.8
Transport equipment	255.3	18.9	48.1	0.928	44.7	170.5	13.8	0.585	28.2	249.2	18.9	47.0	63.5
Miscellaneous manufactures	77.9	11.3	8.8	0.837	7.4	36.2	3.0	0.597	5.3	43.2	11.3	4.9	7.0
Electricity, gas, and water[9]	381.8	1.4	5.2	0.452	2.3	35.9	2.2	0.236	1.2	—	—	—	1.1
Banks, insurance, and services[10]	952.1	2.8	27.1	0.531	14.4	220.2	2.2	0.109	3.0	31.1	—	—	11.4
Communications (telephone)	201.4	6.0	12.1	1.000	12.1	64.9	3.0	0.250	3.0	22.4	6.0	1.3	10.4
Personal services[11]	1,345.4	3.5	46.5	0.470	21.8	419.2	5.1	0.408	19.0	3.4	3.4	0.1	3.0
Retail trade	1,221.1	8.4[12]	102.9	0.670	68.9	461.0	32.7	0.850	87.5	—	—	—	–18.5

Sources: Tax Studies Subdirectorate, Directorate of National Taxes; and IMF staff estimates.

[1] Average of the rate for each range (code) of the sectors. Column 3 is therefore not necessarily equal to the product of column 1 and column 2.

[2] The difference between "gross income" (line 1:BA on the VAT declaration form) and "income from taxed operations" (line 4:BD). This calculation eliminates exports.

[3] (5) = (3) × (4).

[4] Using the input-output matrix of 1988, the specific rate for each of the sector's inputs has been applied to the amount of that input; the total for all is reflected in this column.

[5] (9) = (3) × (8).

[6] If the specific code is obvious, the relevant rate is applied. If not, the effective rate for gross output (column 2) is used.

[7] (13) = (5) − (9) + (12).

[8] It is assumed that this import value is 40 percent of total imports, as the remaining 60 percent is not taxed.

[9] Gas only (output valued at Col$129.071 billion) is included in the base, at a rate of 4 percent.

[10] Insurance only (excluding life insurance) is included in the base (valued at Col$180.8 billion), at a rate of 15 percent.

[11] Two thirds (66 percent) of output was not taxed.

[12] This average has been determined on the basis of commercial markups for all sectors.

Table 24. VAT Credit for Capital Goods of Large Taxpayers in Bogotá
(In billions of Colombian pesos, unless otherwise specified)

Economic Sector	1993 Credit (For 1,332 taxpayers)	1993 Credit (For 1,197 taxpayers)[1]	1992 Credit
Agriculture, forestry, and fishing	0.15	0.15	0.07
Mining	4.68	4.68	0.79
Food products	4.58	4.59	1.35
Textiles and leather	2.64	2.63	0.86
Wood and wood products	0.67	0.67	0.39
Chemical products	3.87	3.87	1.23
Mineral products	4.65	4.65	1.48
Electricity and gas	0.44	0.44	0.19
Construction	0.21	0.21	0.07
Wholesale trade	2.06	2.05	0.74
Retail trade	0.45	0.41	1.18
Transport and communication	0.68	0.68	1.32
Finance	11.78	10.82	3.55
Services	1.56	1.55	0.46
Total	38.42	37.40	13.68

Sources: Large-Taxpayer Unit, National Directorate of Taxes and Customs; and IMF staff estimates.

[1]Even though the actual number of large taxpayers was 1,332 in 1993, 1,197 large taxpayers are used for 1993 to make the results comparable with 1992.

Appendix III   User Cost of Capital

In this appendix, the methodology for computing the user cost of capital in Colombia is developed. One of the ways of defining the user cost of capital is as the "rent" that must be paid to use a unit of capital stock. This definition leads to a measurement of the cost of using capital as

$$CUK = q(R + dep),\qquad(1)$$

where CUK is the user cost of capital; q is the real price of the capital asset; R is the real rate of return obtained by the owner of the asset; and dep is the rate of economic depreciation (percentage of the value of the asset), which is equivalent to the change in the real value of the asset.

As measured by its value, the capital stock would be $q = 1$. In that case, the capital use cost would become

$$CUK = R + dep.\qquad(2)$$

However, the real rate of return obtained by the owner of the asset (R) should be in equilibrium with the rate of return paid both to the firm's creditors (debtor interest) and its shareholders (dividends). The taxation of these payments with regard to both companies and individuals causes a discrepancy among the flows generated in the company, the payments made to creditors and shareholders, and what these two groups actually receive after taxes and commissions.

Situation Prior to the 1986 Reform

Before the 1986 reform, there was double taxation on dividends. The profits of enterprises were taxed (at the rate of 4 percent for corporations and 18 percent for limited companies); once the dividends were distributed after payment of these taxes, individual taxes were levied on them in accordance with a progressive schedule that went up to 49 percent. While companies were not required to pay taxes on interest payments on debts, the persons receiving the interest payments were taxed.

The equilibrium relationships that existed among the different variables related to debt financing are as follows:

$$rho\,D = r\,cap(1 - tp),\text{ and}\qquad(3)$$

$$r\,col = r\,cap + s,\qquad(4)$$

where $rho\,D$ is the after-tax rate of return obtained by individuals; $r\,cap$ is the interest rate paid by financial institutions to individuals (the borrowing rate); tp is the marginal personal tax rate; $r\,col$ is the interest rate charged by financial institutions to enterprises (the lending rate); and s is the gross spread of financial corporations.

The equilibrium relations among the variables involved in financing of enterprises through shares of stock are as follows:

$$rho\,A = rA(1 - div\,tp - (1 - div)tg - mA),\qquad(5)$$

and

$$rho\,A = rho\,D + pr,\qquad(6)$$

where $rho\,A$ is the after-tax rate of return obtained by individuals on their investments in stocks; rA is the rate of return on stock before taxes; div is the percentage of profits distributed as dividends (the dividend policy); tg is the marginal rate of capital gains taxes; mA is the stock exchange commission on buying and selling shares; and pr is the premium for assuming systematic risk of a market portfolio.

The equilibrium relationship among these variables for an enterprise is

$$R = fr\,col + (1 - f)rA/(1 - te) \\ - Zte/(1 - te) - (1 - f)inf\,te/(1 - te),\qquad(7)$$

where f is the debt-assets ratio; te is the profit tax rate for enterprises; Z is the present value of depreciation flow; and inf is the rate of inflation.

Situation After the 1986 Reform

The 1986 reform gradually unified the profit tax rates of corporations and limited companies (at 30 percent the highest bracket of individual income and capital gains taxes). Companies pay the 30 percent tax, and the dividends paid out of the remaining 70 percent are exempt from individual income taxes. Beginning in 1991, the capital gains tax was also eliminated ($tg = 0$). Beginning in 1992, a method for overall adjustment for inflation will be introduced (equivalent to $inf = 0$).

With these changes, the equilibrium relations in debt financing do not change equations (3) and (4). Financing via stock shares is changed as follows:

$$rho\ A = rA(1 - (1 - div)tg - mA). \qquad (5')$$

Equations (6) and (7) do not change.

User Cost of Capital in Colombia

To compute the user cost of capital in Colombia, Harberger's (1969) method was used, which requires construction of a capital stock series. There are various series available. These series include those computed by Harberger himself (1969), García García (1988), and Clavijo (1990).

Clavijo's capital stock series, the most current one for Colombia, probably overestimates the deprecia-

tion rate and thus underestimates the true capital stock. This hypothesis was verified by computing the capital-output ratio, which, in 1989, was 1.7, based on Clavijo's series. As this value seemed too low, an alternative series was computed, based on the assumption of a "one-hoss-shay depreciation" for a period of 30 years. Using this assumption, the capital stock was found to be equal to investment in fixed assets for the previous 30 years.

The capital stock, expressed in millions of constant 1975 Colombian pesos, was valued in nominal terms by using the investment deflator. The user cost of capital was then estimated by dividing gross capital payments by the value of capital stock in nominal terms (see Table 25).

Next, the user cost of capital was adjusted to the borrowing and lending rates by using the previously defined equilibrium equations. For enterprises the average tax rate for corporations and limited companies was used. For individuals, the highest marginal individual income tax bracket was employed.

The results for Colombia and the parameters used in the estimation are shown in Tables 25 through 30.

Table 25. User Cost of Capital
(In billions of Colombian pesos, unless otherwise specified)

Year	Capital Stock (At 1975 prices) (1)	Capital Stock (At current prices) (2)	Capital Payments (At current prices) (3)	Capital Use Cost[1] (In percent) (4)
1970	865,933	457,861	71,040	15.5
1971	903,547	442,201	82,696	18.7
1972	943,069	525,726	102,086	19.4
1973	980,781	633,845	134,630	21.2
1974	1,022,570	836,413	180,232	21.5
1975	1,068,767	1,068,767	220,203	20.6
1976	1,111,659	1,381,767	285,013	20.6
1977	1,159,688	1,760,925	375,517	21.3
1978	1,207,331	2,254,341	449,266	19.9
1979	1,260,522	2,971,202	579,107	19.5
1980	1,315,608	3,959,244	763,762	19.3
1981	1,379,948	5,164,135	966,861	18.7
1982	1,451,313	6,571,740	1,205,800	18.3
1983	1,523,731	8,207,028	1,460,512	17.8
1984	1,588,857	10,540,076	1,823,022	17.3
1985	1,649,892	15,359,338	2,431,847	15.8
1986	1,703,635	20,381,230	3,414,059	16.8
1987	1,766,554	26,762,411	4,439,895	16.6
1988	1,839,736	37,410,326	6,011,023	16.1
1989	1,925,341	49,974,999	7,791,107	15.6

Source: IMF staff estimates.

[1]The user cost of capital was obtained by dividing capital payments at current prices, as indicated in the national accounts (column 3), by the capital stock at current prices (column 2). To compute the latter, the national accounts' investment deflator was used.

Table 26. Rate of Return on Shares
(In percent)

Year	Capital Use Cost (*CUK*)	Depreciation (*dep*)	Real Rate of Return on Capital (*R*)	Real Rate of Return on Capital Stock (*rA*)	Rate of Return on Shares (*rho A*)
1986	16.8	2.2	14.6	26.3	13.0
1987	16.6	1.6	15.0	20.2	19.3
1988	16.1	1.5	14.6	19.3	18.4
1989	15.6	1.5	14.1	17.0	16.3
1990	15.3	1.5	13.8	14.8	14.1
1991	15.2	1.5	13.7	14.9	14.7

Source: IMF staff estimates.

Table 27. Rate of Return on Debt
(In percent)

Year	Real Lending Rate (*r col*)	Real Borrowing Rate (*r cap*)	Gross Spread (*s*)	Real Rate of Return on Debt (*rho D*)
1986	15.3	7.6	7.7	3.9
1987	13.8	5.5	8.3	3.8
1988	11.3	4.1	7.2	2.9
1989	13.4	6.1	7.3	4.2
1990	9.7	3.0	6.7	2.1
1991	11.7	3.9	7.8	2.7

Source: IMF staff estimates.

Table 28. Rates of Taxes and Margins
(In percent)

Year	Stock Exchange Margin (*mA*)	Rate of Enterprise Taxes (*te*)	Rate of Individual Income Taxes (*tp*)	Rate of Capital Gains Tax (*tg*)
1986	1.4	29.0	49.0	49.0
1987	1.4	31.5	30.0	30.0
1988	1.4	31.0	30.0	30.0
1989	1.4	30.5	30.0	30.0
1990	1.4	30.0	30.0	30.0
1991	1.4	30.0	30.0	—

Source: IMF staff estimates.

Table 29. Present Value of Depreciation (Z)
(In percent)

	Without Inflation[1]	10 Percent Annual Inflation	20 Percent Annual Inflation	25 Percent Annual Inflation	30 Percent Annual Inflation
4 years	69.7	56.2	46.6	42.8	39.6
6 years	61.1	46.2	36.5	32.9	29.9
10 years	48.0	32.9	24.5	21.5	19.3
15 years	36.8	23.4	16.8	14.7	13.0
20 years	29.3	17.9	12.7	11.0	9.8
49 years	12.6	7.3	5.2	4.5	4.0
40-40-20 system[2]	76.8	65.4	56.7	53.0	49.8

Source: IMF staff estimates.

[1]With the system for overall inflation adjustment, the same tax effect is achieved as without inflation.

[2]Accelerated depreciation system in which depreciation is 40 percent for the first year and 40 percent for the second year, with the remaining depreciation of 20 percent occurring in the third year.

Table 30. Parameters for Computing the User Cost of Capital
(In percent)

Year	Inflation (inf)	Debt (f)	Present Value of Depreciation (Z)	Dividend Policy (div)
1986	22.2	0.76	20.0	90
1987	24.0	0.61	20.0	90
1988	28.1	0.58	20.0	90
1989	26.1	0.58	20.0	90
1990	32.4	0.50	20.0	90
1991	27.0	0.50	20.0	90

Source: IMF staff estimates.

Appendix IV Disaggregated Investment and Savings Model

Formulation of the Model

A disaggregated model for savings and private investment is developed below. The savings and investment process is put in the context of simultaneous equations, and the selection of variables and definitions is done on the basis of neoclassical guidelines.

Total savings in the economy (S) can be broken down into private savings (Sp), public savings (Sg), and external savings (Se). The latter concept is defined in national terms, so that it coincides with the deficit of the balance of payments on current account:

$$S = Sp + Sg + Se. \qquad (8)$$

Total investment (I) can be broken down into private fixed capital investment (Ip), public fixed capital investment (Ig), and changes in stocks (VE),[51] as follows:

$$I = Ip + Ig + VE. \qquad (9)$$

For the economy to be in equilibrium, total investment must be equal to total savings, namely,

$$I = S. \qquad (10)$$

All the nominal variables (savings, investment, and taxes) are deflated by the gross domestic product, so that they are expressed as percentages of GDP. Private savings (Sp) is modeled in terms of direct taxes (td), indirect taxes (ti), participations in capital holdings (sk), government transfers and interest payments (tr), public savings (Sg), external savings (Se), and the rate of return on savings (rho). These variables take into account the following: the presumably positive stimulus of an increase in the rate of return on savings (rho) on the level of private savings; the impact of taxes (td and ti) on disposable income; the impact of changes in the distribution of income (sk); and possible crowding-out effects on private savings in the event of increases in external savings (Se) and public savings (Sg).

The empirical results in Table 31 indicate that government and external savings crowd out private savings. An increase in external savings (because of a greater inflow of external capital) can reduce private savings for a wide variety of reasons, including greater wealth received, which increases consumption,[52] as follows:

$$Sp = f(sk, ti, td, Sg, Se, rho). \qquad (11)$$

Private investment (Ip) is modeled in terms of the deferred investment during a period ($Ip(-1)$), the cost of using capital (CUK), the real price of capital goods (Pk/P), public investment (Ig), real wages (w/P), and the capital-output ratio (K/Q), as follows:

$$Ip = g(Ip(-1), CUK, Pk/P, Ig, w/P, K/Q). \qquad (12)$$

The user cost of capital (CUK) is equal to the rate of return on savings (rho) plus tax rates and the spread of the financial system.[53] If tax rates and the spread of the financial system are termed the "gap," then

$$CUK = rho + gap. \qquad (13)$$

The change in stocks is related to a lag time of one period ($VE(-1)$) and the growth of output (g):

$$VE = h(VE(-1), g). \qquad (14)$$

The remaining variables are public saving (Sg), external saving (Se), and public investment (Ig),

---

[51]It is impossible to separate clearly the public and private components of changes in stocks in Colombia. Some observers, for example, regard coffee stocks as public, and treat the remainder as private. In this analysis, changes in stocks are not modeled.

[52]As the World Bank (1991, pp. 122–23) notes:
"A World Bank study of [a] sample of developing countries found that less than half of the increase in public saving obtained by cutting government consumption will be offset by lower private saving; in the case of a tax increase, slightly more of the increase in public saving will be offset . . . . A significant share of foreign capital may be used to finance consumption instead of investment, reducing the long-run effect of inflows on growth . . . . The additional consumption spending from an additional dollar of foreign loans in the 1960s and 1970s was 88 cents for Bolivia, and 99 cents for Colombia."

[53]Information as to the derivation of the CUK series is found in Appendix III.

Table 31. Private Savings Equation, 1970–89[1]

		Regression No. 1	Regression No. 2	Regression No. 3	Regression No. 4
Number of observations		20	20	20	20
Degrees of freedom		13	15	15	14
Estimation method		OLS[2]	OLS[2]	TSLS[3]	TSLS[3]
R^2		0.75589	0.75127	0.73114	0.73240
Standard error		0.01116	0.01048	0.01869	0.01138
Constant	a0	0.21450	0.17206	0.15723	0.19550
$sk(1-ti)$	a1	−0.10604			−0.10520
		(−0.496)			(−0.676)
tr	a2	−0.20117			
		(−0.363)			
td	a3	−0.68049	−0.87197	−1.16470	−0.98157
		(−1.213)	(−2.279)	(−2.741)	(−1.973)
Sg	a4	−0.47193	−0.42021	−0.24715	−0.23272
		(−1.478)	(−1.649)	(−0.882)	(−0.802)
Se	a5	−0.46495	−0.43172	−0.28869	−0.28389
		(−2.187)	(−2.468)	(−1.474)	(−1.408)
rho	a6	0.47080	0.39166	0.63037	0.67033
		(1.762)	(2.025)	(2.717)	(2.686)

Source: IMF staff estimates.
[1]t statistics in parentheses.
[2]Ordinary least squares.
[3]Two-stage least squares.

which are regarded as exogenous vis-à-vis the saving and investment sector. They give rise to three additional equations:

$$Sg = Sg \text{ (exogenous variable)}, \quad (15)$$

$$Se = Se \text{ (exogenous variable), and} \quad (16)$$

$$Ig = Ig \text{ (exogenous variable).} \quad (17)$$

It is easy to verify that the private saving and private investment equations are identified, so they can be estimated by two-stage least squares (TSLS) in a consistent way. If they are estimated by ordinary least squares (OLS), the coefficients are subject to a simultaneous-type bias, although they may perform better in small samples (with a lower average standard error).

Application of the Model to Colombia

To estimate the private saving equation, the following equation was estimated for the 1970–89 period:

$$Sp = a0 + a1sk(1-ti) + a2tr + a3td \\ + a4Sg + a5Se + a6rho, \quad (18)$$

where Sp is the private savings rate (in percent of GDP); sk is the capital share of geographic income; ti is indirect taxes less subsidies (in percent of GDP); tr is government transfers and interest payments (in percent of GDP); td is direct taxes (in percent of GDP); Sg is public savings (in percent of GDP); Se is external savings (in percent of GDP); and rho is the real annual rate of return on savings (in percent). The results are indicated in Table 31.

The private investment equation estimated for the period 1970–89 is as follows:

$$Ip = b0 + b1Ip(-1) + b2CUK + b3(Pk/P) \\ + b4Ig + b5(w/P) + b6(K/Q), \quad (19)$$

where Ip is the private investment rate; CUK is the capital use cost; Pk/P is the real price of capital goods; Ig is the public investment rate; w/P is the real wages; and K/Q is the capital-output ratio. The results obtained are indicated in Table 32.

Reduced Form and Evaluation of Impact

If the ratios from the best savings and investment equations estimated with the two-stage least squares method are substituted in equations (8) and (9), the following structural form is obtained to represent the

Table 32. Private Investment Equation, 1970–89[1]

		Regression No. 1	Regression No. 2	Regression No. 3	Regression No. 4
Number of observations		20	20	20	20
Degrees of freedom		13	17	17	16
Estimation method		OLS[2]	OLS[2]	TSLS[3]	OLS[3]
R^2		0.74091	0.70670	0.70644	0.73039
Standard error		0.00662	0.00616	0.00616	0.00609
Constant	b0	0.06338	0.17538	0.17323	0.12908
$Ip(-1)$	b1	0.21230	0.21639	0.22394	0.16935
		(0.930)	(1.102)	(1.099)	(0.855)
CUK	b2	−0.18555	−0.37016	−0.36412	−0.27455
		(−0.472)	(−3.878)	(−3.531)	(−2.212)
Pk/P	b3	0.03169			0.03347
		(0.428)			(1.186)
Ig	b4	0.08039			
		(0.429)			
w/P	b5	0.000001			
		(0.350)			
K/Q	b6	0.00892			
		(0.199)			

Source: IMF staff estimates.
[1] t statistics in parentheses.
[2] Ordinary least squares.
[3] Two-stage least squares.

total investment and saving market in Colombia in the short term:

$$S = 0.15723 - 1.16470td + 0.75284Sg + 0.71131Se + 0.63037rho,$$
$$I = 0.17323 + 0.22394Ip(-1) + Ig - 0.36412CUK + c0 + c1VE(-1) + c2g,$$
$$CUK = rho + gap, \text{ and}$$
$$S = I.$$

Coefficients c0, c1, and c2 correspond to the regression on the change in stocks (which is not required to obtain the desired impact). Solving the system of structural equations on the basis of the endogenous variables (S, I, rho, and CUK), the following reduced form for the short-term impact is obtained:

$$S = I = 0.16737 - 0.42644td + 0.27564Sg + 0.26043Se + 0.23080gap + 0.14194Ip(-1) + 0.63386Ig + 0.63386c0 + 0.63386c1VE(-1) + 0.63386c2g,$$
$$CUK = 0.01608 + 1.17115td - 0.75702Sg - 0.71525Se - 0.63386gap + 0.22518Ip(-1) + 1.00554Ig + 1.00554c0 + 1.00554c1VE(-1) + 1.00554g, \text{ and}$$
$$rho = CUK - gap.$$

If private investment is equivalent to its deferred value (that is, if $Ip = Ip(-1)$), and if the latter variable is substituted in the structural equations, the long-term impact of the structural variables on savings, investment, and the user cost of capital can be determined. This is obtained in the following reduced form for the long-term impact:

$$S = I = 0.19505 - 0.49698td + 0.32124Sg + 0.30352Se + 0.26898gap + 0.57329Ig + 0.57329c0/(1-c1) + 0.57329gc2/(1-c1), \text{ and}$$
$$CUK = 0.06001 + 1.05924td - 0.68468Sg - 0.64690Se - 0.57329gap + 0.90945Ig + 0.90945c0/(1-c1) + 0.90945gc2/(1-c1).$$

From these reduced forms, the impact of certain variables on the rate of total investment and savings in the Colombian economy can be evaluated (Table 33).

It is also possible to use this model to evaluate the short- and long-term impact that the reduction in the tax gap had on the investment rate. As a result of the elimination of double taxation and the reduction in the tax rates, the gap was reduced from 10.7 percent in 1986 to 6.3 percent in 1989. When this reduction is applied to the reduced form, the impacts described in Table 34 can be obtained.

Table 33. Estimated Impact of Change in Variables on the Investment Rate
(In percent of GDP)

1 Percent GDP Change in Variable	Effect on Total Investment (Short-term)	Effect on Total Investment (Long-term)	Effect on Private Savings (Long-term)	Effect on Private Investment (Long-term)
Increase in direct taxes (keeping public savings constant)	−0.43	−0.50	−0.50	−0.50
Increase in direct taxes (increasing public savings with these resources)	−0.15	−0.18	−1.18	−0.18
Increase in direct taxes (increasing public investment with these resources)	0.21	0.08	−0.92	−0.92
Reduction in public savings	−0.28	−0.32	0.68	−0.32
Reduction in external savings	−0.26	−0.30	0.70	−0.30

Source: IMF staff estimates.

Table 34. Estimated Impact on Variables of Reduction in Tax Gap, 1986–89
(In percent of GDP, unless otherwise specified)

Variable	Short-Term Impact	Long-Term Impact
Total investment rate	1.0	1.2
Private investment rate	1.0	1.2
Private saving rate	1.0	1.2
Capital user cost (real annual percent change)	−2.8	−2.5
Rate of return on savings (real annual percent change)	1.6	1.9

Source: IMF staff estimates.

Appendix V   Adjustments Needed to Obtain Potential Income Tax Base

This appendix presents technical details of adjustments made to the gross operating surplus (*EBE*) that are necessary to obtain the potential income tax base. First, the national accounts provide information on the *EBE* from nonfinancial corporations, financial institutions, the Government, and families. This information enables the *EBE* to be allocated between corporations and individuals independently of the tax return data. The amount adjusted for implicit rental income of owner-occupied housing is then removed from the *EBE* assigned to individuals.[54] However, it is less clear how the *EBE* should be adjusted for the informal economy. For instance, the adjustment of the national accounts may be measuring elements that do not belong in the tax base, such as subsistence farming, in which case they should be removed for the purposes of this exercise. It is also possible that this adjustment reflects an estimate of tax evasion itself. In this case, the estimate should be included in the measure for potential taxable income, but care should be taken that it is fairly consistent with the results obtained in the study.[55]

The adjustment made for interest earnings is also tricky. To some extent, interest earned and interest paid offset each other in the aggregated calculation. However, the offset deteriorates if interest earnings and interest payments are taxed asymmetrically or if much of the interest earnings accrue to individuals, who are taxed at different rates than corporations. In any case, if interest deductions are included in the calculations, the *EBE* must be adjusted for interest earned. It is important to note that the Center for Fiscal Studies did not make this adjustment. The interest earnings adjustments shown in Table 35 are

based on data from the national accounts. Other sources of information that may be worth investigating are records from the central bank and the supervisor of the banking system. Of particular interest are the stock of deposits, as well as interest earning assets of firms and individuals and their yields. Also, because of inflation adjustments in the calculation of taxable income, interest earned must be lowered accordingly for the purposes of this study.

With respect to costs and deductions, it is necessary to estimate interest deductions and allowances for depreciation and depletion allowances. Again, data from the national accounts have been used for interest paid, but more up-to-date information is probably available from the central bank or the supervisor of the banking system. It should be emphasized that, to obtain the appropriate tax deduction, interest payments are subject to the inflation adjustment. It is also important to distinguish between interest deductions for corporations and individuals. As it is quite likely that corporations have much greater access to the credit market than do individuals, this deduction would be disproportionately allocated to corporations.

The measurement of depreciation allowances is an involved procedure. However, it is important and it can be done, as evidenced by Table 36. Essentially, given the data on investment in the national accounts, the rules for depreciation can be applied directly to obtain an insightful estimate. Until 1992, the "40-40-20" method was available for assets other than buildings. For buildings (and other construction), the double-declining balance method has been used in conjunction with a switch-over mechanism to fully depreciate the asset. These methods have been applied to the historical costs.[56]

---

[54]Explicit data for this adjustment were not available. The figure used in this exercise is only an illustration and is equal to 5 percent of the *EBE* for individuals.

[55]In the absence of further information, the *EBE* is not adjusted for tax evasion.

---

[56]Corporations account for a disproportionate share of investment.

Table 35. Calculation of Adjusted Income for Income Tax
(In millions of current Colombian pesos, unless otherwise specified)

	1987	1988	1989	1990	1991	1992
(1) Gross operating surplus (*EBE*) from national accounts	4,439,895	6,011,023	7,742,394	10,638,836	13,877,317	18,107,278
(a) Enterprises	1,974,235	2,631,448	3,532,930	4,909,261	6,403,649	8,355,553
(b) Financial institutions	−114,358	−195,443	−238,321	−272,558	−355,525	−463,893
(c) Households	2,789,242	3,629,345	4,519,798	6,121,833	7,985,330	10,419,348
(d) Public administration	−209,224	−54,327	−72,013	−119,700	−156,137	−203,729
(2) Less implicit rent from owner-occupied housing[1]	139,462	181,467	225,990	306,092	399,267	520,967
(3) Less GDP adjustment for illegal activities	—	—	—	—	—	—
(4) Less GDP adjustment for other activities not subject to income tax[2]	1,394,621	1,814,673	2,259,899	3,060,917	3,992,665	5,209,674
(5) Plus taxable interest earned	1,122,321	1,634,558	2,354,564	3,141,586	4,097,890	5,346,973
(a) Enterprises	139,113	216,315	283,760	408,543	532,904	695,339
(b) Financial institutions	667,774	995,616	1,490,210	1,935,438	2,524,589	3,294,112
(c) Households	315,434	422,627	580,594	797,605	1,040,397	1,357,522
(6) Inflation adjustment (in percent)	12.92	20.00	20.73	30.00	40.00	50.00
(7) Equals adjusted income for taxes						
(a) Corporations $=((1a)+(1b)+(5a)+(5b)) \times (100-(6))$	2,562,514	3,405,550	4,700,835	6,277,490	7,882,620	9,886,385
(b) Individuals $=((1c)-(2)-(4)+(5c)) \times (100-(6))$	1,570,593	2,055,832	2,614,503	3,552,430	4,633,796	6,046,229

Sources: Data provided by authorities; and IMF staff estimates.

[1]This adjustment is estimated to be 5 percent of the *EBE* of households. The actual adjustment can be obtained from the National Administrative Department of Statistics (DANE).

[2]For example, DANE makes adjustments for the informal sector. To the extent that the informal sector, such as subsistence agriculture, is not subject to income tax, this adjustment should be removed from potential taxable income. These issues should be discussed in-depth with DANE; in this case, the adjustment is assumed to be 50 percent of the *EBE* of households.

Table 36. Calculation of Depreciation Allowances for Income Tax
(In millions of current Colombian pesos)

	1987	1988	1989	1990	1991	1992
Corporations						
Buildings (20-year useful life)						
(1) New investment	387,239	656,944	701,001	774,382	1,010,105	1,317,996
(2) Expired basis	...	127,601	166,262	216,427	266,712	326,667
(3) Current basis	1,301,540	1,696,031	2,208,741	2,730,006	3,355,537	4,192,921
(4) Depreciation allowance $=.10(3_t)$	130,154	169,603	220,874	273,001	335,554	419,292
Machinery and equipment (10-year useful life)						
(5) New investment	320,061	449,578	574,559	817,841	1,066,794	1,391,965
(6) Depreciation allowances $=.20(5_t)+.40(5_{t-1})+.40(5_{t-2})$	216,247	307,491	422,767	573,223	770,319	823,452
Vehicles (5-year useful life)						
(7) New investment	168,151	253,613	260,309	336,499	438,930	572,720
(8) Depreciation allowances $=.20(7_t)+.40(7_{t-1})+.40(7_{t-2})$	103,532	159,980	220,767	272,868	326,509	367,443
(9) Total depreciation $=(4_t)+(6_t)+(8_t)$	449,933	637,074	864,409	1,119,092	1,432,382	1,610,187
Depletion allowances						
(10) Production (mining sector)	577,797	722,193	1,157,936	1,765,149	2,302,464	3,004,280
(11) Depreciation allowance $=.10(10_t)$	57,780	72,219	115,794	176,515	230,246	300,428
Individuals						
Buildings (20-year useful life)						
(12) New investment	60,755	95,164	108,332	123,163	160,653	209,622
(13) Expired basis	...	17,471	23,289	30,812	38,847	48,532
(14) Current basis	182,090	242,579	321,038	405,972	509,033	645,639
(15) Depreciation allowance $=.10(14_t)$	18,209	24,258	32,104	40,597	50,903	64,564
Machinery and equipment (10-year useful life)						
(16) New investment	50,215	65,126	88,792	130,075	169,670	221,387
(17) Depreciation allowances $=.20(16_t)+.40(16_{t-1})+.40(16_{t-2})$	25,928	43,598	63,895	87,582	121,480	130,967
Vehicles (5-year useful life)						
(18) New investment	26,382	36,738	40,228	53,519	69,810	91,089
(19) Depreciation allowances $=.20(18_t)+.40(18_{t-1})+.40(18_{t-2})$	12,597	22,818	33,293	41,490	51,461	58,440
(20) Total depreciation $=(15_t)+(17_t)+(19_t)$	56,735	90,674	129,292	169,669	223,844	253,971

Source: IMF staff estimates.

Appendix VI   Customs Tariffs: Computing the Change in Fiscal Receipts

When there is a change in a tariff (from t_0 to t_1) on a product whose international price is p, the domestic price changes from $p(1 + t_0)$ to $p(1 + t_1)$, and the amount demanded changes from q_0 to q_1, according to the price elasticity of the demand for that product.[57] If $t_0 > t_1$, the domestic price will go down along with the new tariff, and the amount demanded will go up, namely, $q_0 < q_1$. Fiscal receipts will thus undergo two opposite effects: they will decrease by $p(t_0 - t_1)q_0$, before increasing by $pt_1(q_1 - q_0)$.

The change in receipts, $dRec$, can be expressed by putting the two effects together with their respective signs:

$$dRec = pt_1(q_1 - q_0) - p(t_0 - t_1)q_0.$$

However, pq_0 is the c.i.f. value of imports of the product in question, before the change in tariffs. If $CIF = pq_0$, the equation can be written as

$$dRec = CIF(t_0 - t_1)\left(\frac{t_1(q_1 - q_0)}{q_0(t_0 - t_1)} - 1\right). \quad (20)$$

If N represents the price elasticity of demand,

$$N = \frac{(q_1 - q_0)(1 + t_0)}{-(t_0 - t_1)q_0}.$$

Then, equation (20) can be written as

$$dRec = CIF\left(\frac{-Nt_1}{1 + t_0} - 1\right)(t_0 - t_1), \quad (21)$$

which is the same formula used in the text of this paper.

It should be noted that $dRec = 0$ if CIF is zero, or if $t_0 = t_1$. In other words, fiscal receipts do not vary if there is no change in the tariff (that is, if $t_0 = t_1$), or if the change affects a product that is not imported. We can also obtain $dRec = 0$, if $N = -(1 + t_0)/t_1$. Fiscal receipts thus do not change if the demand elasticity is such that the two offsetting effects mentioned earlier cancel each other out.

It can also be observed in equation (21) that if the elasticity is zero (that is, if the amount of the product demanded does not respond to the change in the tariff), the second fiscal receipts effect disappears, and the change in fiscal receipts becomes maximal, as the effects no longer offset each other. In that case,

$$dRec = CIF(t_0 - t_1).$$

Equation (21) shows that fiscal receipts could *increase* when tariffs *decrease*, and vice versa. This situation occurs whenever the second effect prevails over the first, namely, when the demand response of the product to the tariff change is stronger than the decrease in the receipts on the amount of the product initially demanded. This occurs whenever demand elasticity, in absolute terms, is greater than $(1 + t_0)/t_1$. For most tariff changes, this result is extremely rare. For instance, if tariffs are reduced from 20 percent to 10 percent, receipts increase only if demand elasticity, in absolute terms, exceeds 12, which is an unusually high demand elasticity for most products.

This computation was done for each of the 4,700 tariff items for which there were imports, converted from the NABANDINA (or Brussels nomenclature) to the NANDINA (or S.I.T.C. nomenclature), so as to use c.i.f. values for 1990 imports. In this study, the tariff items were grouped into 16 categories, with the results shown in Table 37. The estimation procedure consisted in adopting for each category two demand elasticity values: one considered arbitrarily low, which overestimates the fiscal cost of the tariff reduction and leads to a "pessimistic evaluation"; and the other arbitrarily high, which thereby underestimates the fiscal cost of the tariff reduction and produces an "optimistic evaluation."

Relatively low values were selected for those products that do not have good substitutes, such as foodstuffs, fuel, and chemical products (groups 1, 3, and 4 in Table 37). Higher values were chosen for products not regarded as essential, such as precious metals and stones, and surface, air, and water vehicles (groups 11, 14, and 15 in Table 37).

---

[57]For practical purposes, the cross-effects that changes in prices of other products could have on the demand for the product analyzed can be ignored. Owing to the insufficiency of data in practice, the omission of cross-effects appears to be a comparatively insignificant error.

Table 37. Estimation of Annual Change in Collections of Tariffs and Surcharges in 1992, Based on Alternative Demand Elasticity Values (in 1990 Prices)

| | Elasticities | | Changes in Collections (In millions of Colombian pesos) | |
Chapter Groups	Low	High	Pessimistic evaluation	Optimistic evaluation
1. Food and animal and vegetable products, Chapters 1–22	−0.5	−1.5	−13,430	−11,443
2. Miscellaneous, Chapters 23–26	−1.0	−2.0	−1,709	−1,555
3. Fuels, Chapter 27	−0.3	−1.0	−3,933	−3,477
4. Chemical products, Chapters 28–38	−0.3	−1.5	−29,629	−26,485
5. Plastic and rubber products, Chapters 39–40	−1.0	−3.0	−12,374	−9,652
6. Leather products and skins, Chapters 41–43	−1.5	−4.0	−324	−205
7. Forestry products, Chapters 44–47	−0.7	−2.0	−1,380	−1,183
8. Paper products, Chapters 48–49	−1.0	−3.0	−5,719	−4,577
9. Clothing and textiles, Chapters 50–67	−0.5	−2.0	−11,507	−9,614
10. Nonmetallic mineral products, Chapters 68–70	−0.7	−2.0	−2,599	−2,255
11. Precious metals and stones, Chapter 71	−2.0	−4.0	−76	−53
12. Metallic products, Chapters 72–81	−0.7	−2.0	−13,981	−12,087
13. Tools and machinery, Chapters 82–85	−0.7	−2.0	−32,091	−27,132
14. Land vehicles, Chapters 86–87	−1.5	−4.0	−8,714	−4,559
15. Air and water vehicles, Chapters 88–89	−2.0	−4.0	−1,276	−1,015
16. Miscellaneous products, Chapters 90–99	−1.0	−2.0	−7,166	−6,393
Total			−145,908	−121,685

Source: IMF staff estimates.

It bears noting that because the true values of the elasticities are not known, very disparate values were selected for *N* in making the calculations in Table 37.[58] Nonetheless, the results obtained are fairly robust in that they are not highly sensitive to changes in the assumed elasticity values. For example, for group 1 in Table 37 (food and animal and vegetable products), the elasticity values adopted (−0.5 and −1.5) differed by a factor of 3, but the estimates of forgone receipts differed by only 17 percent (Col$13.4 billion versus Col$11.4 billion).

Table 37 shows that the greatest losses in collections were for chemical products (Col$29.6 billion and Col$26.5 billion, according to the pessimistic and optimistic estimations, respectively) and for tools and machinery (Col$32.1 billion and Col$27.1 billion, respectively, depending on the assumptions used). The total revenue forgone was estimated to be between Col$121.7 billion and Col$145.9 billion for 1992, the only year in which the loss was significant.

The totals shown at the bottom of Table 37 are expressed in 1990 prices, since the c.i.f. values of imports used are for that year. To make these figures comparable with those of the National Planning Department and the Ministry of Finance, the estimates

had to be expressed in 1992 prices. This was done by using projected devaluation rates based on National Planning Department and Ministry of Finance estimates (22.3 percent for 1991 and 17.3 percent for 1992). As a result, the revenue collections forgone at 1992 prices in 1992 were estimated to range between Col$174.6 billion and Col$209.4 billion. It bears noting that the estimate by the National Planning Department and Finance Ministry (Col$186 billion for 1992) fell between the pessimistic and optimistic values of the staff's estimation.

In Table 38, the figures in Table 37 were recalculated using only a single, 8 percent surcharge, instead of the three values (zero percent, 5 percent, and 8 percent) in effect in 1991. Expressing the totals shown in Table 38 in 1992 prices (by once again using the devaluation rates projected for 1991 and 1992), the 1992 fiscal cost would be either Col$168.7 billion or Col$141.6 billion, depending on whether pessimistic or optimistic assumptions were used. These values are approximately 20 percent (or Col$35 billion) less than those estimated in Table 37, which used surcharges of zero percent, 5 percent, and 8 percent.

As noted in Section IV, Table 39 provides information on tax reimbursement certificates (CERTs) issued, and Table 40 summarizes the legal provisions affecting import exemptions.

[58]The use of closer values would be tantamount to assuming that the true elasticity value was known. If this were the case, however, it would not be necessary to perform the simulation.

Table 38. Estimation of Annual Change in Collections of Tariffs and Surcharges in 1992, Based on Alternative Demand Elasticity Values and a Uniform Surcharge of 8 Percent (in 1990 Prices)

		Elasticities		Changes in Collections (In millions of Colombian pesos)	
Chapter Groups		Low	High	Pessimistic evaluation	Optimistic evaluation
1.	Food and animal and vegetable products, Chapters 1–22	−0.5	−1.5	−6,174	−5,862
2.	Miscellaneous, Chapters 23–26	−1.0	−2.0	−1,149	−1,225
3.	Fuels, Chapter 27	−0.3	−1.0	−3,933	−3,477
4.	Chemical products, Chapters 28–38	−0.3	−1.5	−18,931	−17,200
5.	Plastic and rubber products, Chapters 39–40	−1.0	−3.0	−6,536	−5,271
6.	Leather products and skins, Chapters 41–43	−1.5	−4.0	−324	−205
7.	Forestry products, Chapters 44–47	−0.7	−2.0	−1,380	−1,183
8.	Paper products, Chapters 48–49	−1.0	−3.0	−4,904	−3,910
9.	Clothing and textiles, Chapters 50–67	−0.5	−2.0	−10,788	−8,924
10.	Nonmetallic mineral products, Chapters 68–70	−0.7	−2.0	−2,599	−2,255
11.	Precious metals and stones, Chapter 71	−2.0	−4.0	−76	−53
12.	Metallic products, Chapters 72–81	−0.7	−2.0	−12,282	−10,672
13.	Tools and machinery, Chapters 82–85	−0.7	−2.0	−31,875	−26,941
14.	Land vehicles, Chapters 86–87	−1.5	−4.0	−8,427	−4,334
15.	Air and water vehicles, Chapters 88–89	−2.0	−4.0	−1,069	−819
16.	Miscellaneous products, Chapters 90–99	−1.0	−2.0	−7,166	−6,394
	Total			−117,613	−98,724

Source: IMF staff estimates.

Table 39. Tax Reimbursement Certificates (CERTs) Issued
(In thousands of Colombian pesos)

City	First Half of 1990	Second Half of 1990	Total 1990	First Half of 1991	July 1991	August 1991
Bogotá	7,137,174	10,039,872	17,177,046	6,499,524	5,282,761	4,086,309
Barranquilla	7,398,560	7,582,470	14,981,030	9,773,920	1,751,810	910,415
Bucaramanga	197,089	263,525	460,614	233,850	233,400	108,540
Buenaventura	508,680	427,105	935,785	505,705	128,965	168,075
Cali	6,800,345	8,152,520	14,952,865	6,647,430	2,796,085	2,033,130
Cartagena	2,222,714	2,482,928	4,705,642	3,260,609	1,099,827	773,931
Cúcuta	793,865	671,245	1,465,110	843,710	483,760	403,750
Leticia						
Manizales	395,030	571,530	966,560	498,230	287,965	206,870
Medellín	4,198,851	6,377,495	10,576,346	5,855,495	3,438,155	1,233,395
Pasto	2,760	5,960	8,720	4,300		315
Pereira	281,042	491,455	772,497	747,660	167,995	98,365
Riohacha						
Santa Marta	145,340	275,785	421,125	245,030	45,260	238,410
Valledupar						
Tunja						
Neiva						
Armenia	4,695	19,195	23,890	73,170	7,015	9,735
Ibague	363,930	480,965	844,895	857,500	189,205	46,355
San Andrés	85,340	212,755	298,095	306,570	73,335	231,255
Ipiales						1,085
Total	30,535,415	38,054,805	68,590,220	36,352,703	15,985,538	10,549,935

Source: Bank of the Republic.

Table 40. Legal Provisions Concerning Import Exemptions

Law	Beneficiary	Exemptions		
		Duty	Surcharge	VAT
Law No. 74/58	Publishing industry	yes	no	no
Decree No. 709/64	Donations related to food shortages	yes	no	no
Decree No. 1659/64	Catholic Church, drugs, vaccinations, Red Cross serum, National Federation of Blind and Deaf-Mutes, oil drilling equipment, mining companies, and the coal industry	yes	no	no
Decree No. 2031/66	Publishing companies	yes	yes	no
Decree No. 232/67	Diplomats	yes	yes	yes
Decree No. 444/67, Article No. 172	Vallejo Plan	yes	yes	yes
Decree No. 444/67, Article No. 173	Vallejo Plan	yes	yes	yes
Decree No. 444/67, Article No. 174	Vallejo Plan	yes	yes	yes
Decree No. 444/67, Article No. 179	Vallejo Plan	yes	yes	yes
Decree No. 1247/69	Raw materials and intermediate goods	yes	yes	no
Decree No. 363/73	Donations to charities	yes	yes	yes
Decree No. 2368/74	Exemption for IMPOVENTAS	no	no	yes
Decree No. 2367/74	Mining and hydrocarbon companies	yes	no	no
Decree No. 314/75	Machinery and equipment used in mining operations	yes	yes	no
Decree No. 584/75	Machinery and equipment used in mining operations	yes	yes	no
Decree No. 2696/76	Petrochemical industry program	no	yes	no
Decree No. 1047/77	Imports to San Andrés	yes	yes	yes
Law No. 18/78	Government treaties	...	...	...
Decree No. 218/78	International agreements	...	...	...
Decree No. 3541/83	Merchandise in Tariff Chapters 01 to 96	no	no	yes
Decree No. 3830/85	Merchandise imported by Nevado del Ruiz Reconstruction Fund	yes	yes	yes
Circular Letter No. 984/86	Exceptions to payment of the surcharge established by Law No. 75/86	no	yes	no
Decree No. 984/86	Mining sector	yes	yes	no
Decree No. 2477/86	Mining sector	yes	yes	no
Decree No. 1013/87	Merchandise from Brazil (Latin American Integration Association (LAIA))	yes	no	no
Decree No. 1722/87	Fuels, oils, etc., imported by selected entities	yes	yes	yes
Decree No. 2583/88	Merchandise from Mexico (LAIA)	yes	no	no
Decree No. 2655/88	Mining sector	yes	no	no
Decree No. 466/88	Merchandise from Argentina (LAIA)	yes	no	no
Decree No. 2051/86	Merchandise from Uruguay (LAIA)	yes	no	no
Decree No. 624/89	Merchandise to San Andrés	yes	yes	yes
Decree No. 731/90	...	no	no	yes

Source: Ministry of Finance.

Bibliography

Aguirre, Carlos, and Parthasarathi Shome, "The Mexican Value-Added Tax (VAT): Methodology for Calculating the Base," *National Tax Journal*, Vol. 41 (December 1988), pp. 543–54.

Carrizosa, Mauricio, *Hacia la Recuperación del Mercado de Capitales de Colombia* (Bogotá: Editorial Presencia Ltda, 1986).

Clavijo, Sergio, "Productividad Laboral, Multifactorial y la Tasa de Cambio Real in Colombia," *Ensayos Sobre Política Económica*, No. 17 (June 1990), pp. 73–97.

Directorate of National Taxes, *Evasion de los Impuestos de Renta y Ventas en Colombia* (Bogotá: Directorate of National Taxes, 1992).

———, "Estimaciones de la Evasion en Colombia," paper presented at Fifth Regional Seminar on Fiscal Policy, United Nations Economic Commission for Latin America and the Caribbean (CEPAL), Santiago, Chile, January 1993.

Edwards, Sebastian, "Coffee, Money and Inflation in Colombia," *World Development*, Vol. 12 (November/December 1984), pp. 1107–17.

Einaudi, Luigi, *Miti e Paradossi della Giustizia Tributaria* (Turin, Italy: Giulio Einaudi, 1959).

Feige, Edgar, "The Meaning and Measurement of the Unobserved Economy," in *The Underground Economies: Tax Evasion and Information Distortion*, ed. by Edgar Feige (Cambridge: Cambridge University Press, 1989).

Garay, Luis J., *Apertura y Protección: Evaluación de la Política de Importaciones* (Bogotá: Tercer Mundo Editores, 1991).

García García, Jorge, "The Timing and Sequencing of a Trade Liberalization Policy: Colombia" (unpublished; World Bank, 1988).

———, and Gabriel Montes Llamas, *Trade, Exchange Rates, and Agricultural Pricing Policies in Colombia*, World Bank Comparative Studies (Washington: World Bank, 1989).

Gillis, Malcolm, and Charles E. McLure, "Coordination of Tariffs and Internal Indirect Taxes," in *Fiscal Reform for Colombia*, ed. by Richard Musgrave and Malcolm Gillis (Cambridge, Massachusetts: Harvard Law School International Tax Program, 1971).

Hallberg, Kristin, and Wendy E. Takacs, "Trade Reform in Colombia, 1990–94," in *The Colombian Economy: Issues of Trade and Development*, ed. by Alvin Cohen and Frank Gunter (Boulder: Westview Press, 1992).

Harberger, Arnold, "La Tasa de Rendimiento del Capital en Colombia," *Revista de Planeación y Desarrollo*, Vol. 1 (October 1969), pp. 13–42.

———, *Taxation and Welfare* (Boston: Little, Brown, 1974).

Herschel, Federico J., *Ensayos Sobre Política Fiscal* (Madrid: Editoriales de Derecho Reunidas, 1975).

International Monetary Fund, "Technical Assistance on Tax Policy: A Review," IMF Working Paper, WP/93/65 (Washington: International Monetary Fund, August 1993).

Lewin, Alfredo, and Horacio Ayala, *Tax Code and Foreign Investment Laws: Colombia, 1990* (Bogotá: Taxworld, 1990).

Lora, Eduardo, *Apertura y Modernización: Las Reformas de los Noventa* (Bogotá: Tercer Mundo Editores, 1991).

McLure, Charles E., "Analysis and Reform of the Colombian Tax System," Working Papers in Economics No. E-88-15/3 (Stanford, California: The Hoover Institution, Stanford University, March 1988).

Musgrave, Richard, and Malcolm Gillis, *Fiscal Reform for Colombia* (Cambridge, Massachusetts: Harvard Law School International Tax Program, 1971).

National Administrative Department of Statistics, *Cuentas Nacionales de Colombia, 1965–1986* (Bogotá: National Administrative Department of Statistics, 1988).

———, *Cuentas Nacionales de Colombia, 1970–1989* (Bogotá: National Administrative Department of Statistics, 1991).

Ocampo, José Antonio, "Determinantes y Perspectivas del Crecimiento Económico en el Mediano Plazo," in *Apertura y Crecimiento: el Rol de los Noventa*, ed. by Eduardo Lora (Bogotá: Tercer Mundo Editores, 1991).

———, "Perspectivas de Crecimiento de la Economía Colombiana," *Coyuntura Economica*, Vol. 22 (July 1992), pp. 113–24.

Price Waterhouse, *Corporate Taxes: A Worldwide Summary* (New York: Price Waterhouse, 1986, 1989, and 1992).

———, *Individual Taxes: A Worldwide Summary* (New York: Price Waterhouse, 1986, 1989, and 1992).

Sadka, Efraim, and Vito Tanzi, "A Tax on Gross Assets of Enterprises as a Form of Presumptive Taxation," *Bulletin for International Fiscal Documentation*, Vol. 47 (February 1993), pp. 66–73.

Sanchez Torres, Fabio, and Catalina Gutiérrez Sourdis, "Casos de Exito en Reformas Fiscales: Colombia, 1980–1992," paper presented at Sixth Regional Seminar on Fiscal Policy, United Nations Economic Commission for Latin America and the Caribbean (CEPAL), Santiago, Chile, January 1994.

Shome, Parthasarathi, "Trends and Future Directions in Tax Policy Reform: A Latin American Perspective," *Bulletin for International Fiscal Documentation*, Vol. 46 (September 1992), pp. 452–66.

———, and Christian Schutte, "Cash-Flow Tax," *Staff Papers*, International Monetary Fund, Vol. 40 (September 1993), pp. 638–62.

Tanzi, Vito, "Fiscal Reform for Colombia: The Report of the Musgrave Commission," *Inter-American Economic Affairs*, Vol. 26 (Summer 1972), pp. 71–80.

———, "Potential Income as a Tax Base in Theory and Practice," in *Public Finance in Developing Countries* (Brookfield, Vermont: Edward Elgar, 1991).

———, "The IMF and Tax Reform," in *Tax Policy and Planning in Developing Countries*, ed. by Amaresh Bagchi and Nicholas Stern (New York: Oxford University Press, 1994).

———, and Ke-young Chu, "La Política Fiscal para un Crecimiento Estable y Equitativo en América Latina," in *Los Problemas del Desarollo en América Latina: Homenaje a Raúl Prebisch*, ed. by Luisa Montuschi and Hans Singer (Buenos Aires: Fondo de Cultura Económica de Argentina, 1992).

———, and Parthasarathi Shome, "A Primer on Tax Evasion," *Staff Papers*, International Monetary Fund, Vol. 40 (December 1993), pp. 328–37.

Wiesner, Eduardo, *Colombia: Descentralización y Federalismo Fiscal: Informe Final de la Mision para la Descentralización* (Bogotá: National Planning Department, 1992).

World Bank, and Jose B. Sokol, *Colombia: Economic Development and Policy under Changing Conditions* (Washington: World Bank, 1984).

———, *World Development Report 1991* (New York: Oxford University Press, 1991).

Recent Occasional Papers of the International Monetary Fund

123. Comprehensive Tax Reform: The Colombian Experience, edited by Parthasarathi Shome. 1995

122. Capital Flows in the APEC Region, edited by Mohsin S. Khan and Carmen M. Reinhart. 1995.

121. Uganda: Adjustment with Growth, 1987–94, by Robert L. Sharer, Hema R. De Zoysa, and Calvin A. McDonald. 1995.

120. Economic Dislocation and Recovery in Lebanon, by Sena Eken, Paul Cashin, S. Nuri Erbas, Jose Martelino, and Adnan Mazarei. 1995.

119. Singapore: A Case Study in Rapid Development, edited by Kenneth Bercuson with a staff team comprising Robert G. Carling, Aasim M. Husain, Thomas Rumbaugh, and Rachel van Elkan. 1995.

118. Sub-Saharan Africa: Growth, Savings, and Investment, by Michael T. Hadjimichael, Dhaneshwar Ghura, Martin Mühleisen, Roger Nord, and E. Murat Uçer. 1995.

117. Resilience and Growth Through Sustained Adjustment: The Moroccan Experience, by Saleh M. Nsouli, Sena Eken, Klaus Enders, Van-Can Thai, Jörg Decressin, and Filippo Cartiglia, with Janet Bungay. 1995.

116. Improving the International Monetary System: Constraints and Possibilities, by Michael Mussa, Morris Goldstein, Peter B. Clark, Donald J. Mathieson, and Tamim Bayoumi. 1994.

115. Exchange Rates and Economic Fundamentals: A Framework for Analysis, by Peter B. Clark, Leonardo Bartolini, Tamim Bayoumi, and Steven Symansky. 1994.

114. Economic Reform in China: A New Phase, by Wanda Tseng, Hoe Ee Khor, Kalpana Kochhar, Dubravko Mihaljek, and David Burton. 1994.

113. Poland: The Path to a Market Economy, by Liam P. Ebrill, Ajai Chopra, Charalambos Christofides, Paul Mylonas, Inci Otker, and Gerd Schwartz. 1994.

112. The Behavior of Non-Oil Commodity Prices, by Eduardo Borensztein, Mohsin S. Khan, Carmen M. Reinhart, and Peter Wickham. 1994.

111. The Russian Federation in Transition: External Developments, by Benedicte Vibe Christensen. 1994.

110. Limiting Central Bank Credit to the Government: Theory and Practice, by Carlo Cottarelli. 1993.

109. The Path to Convertibility and Growth: The Tunisian Experience, by Saleh M. Nsouli, Sena Eken, Paul Duran, Gerwin Bell, and Zühtü Yücelik. 1993.

108. Recent Experiences with Surges in Capital Inflows, by Susan Schadler, Maria Carkovic, Adam Bennett, and Robert Kahn. 1993.

107. China at the Threshold of a Market Economy, by Michael W. Bell, Hoe Ee Khor, and Kalpana Kochhar with Jun Ma, Simon N'guiamba, and Rajiv Lall. 1993.

106. Economic Adjustment in Low-Income Countries: Experience Under the Enhanced Structural Adjustment Facility, by Susan Schadler, Franek Rozwadowski, Siddharth Tiwari, and David O. Robinson. 1993.

105. The Structure and Operation of the World Gold Market, by Gary O'Callaghan. 1993.

104. Price Liberalization in Russia: Behavior of Prices, Household Incomes, and Consumption During the First Year, by Vincent Koen and Steven Phillips. 1993.

103. Liberalization of the Capital Account: Experiences and Issues, by Donald J. Mathieson and Liliana Rojas-Suárez. 1993.

102. Financial Sector Reforms and Exchange Arrangements in Eastern Europe. Part I: Financial Markets and Intermediation, by Guillermo A. Calvo and Manmohan S. Kumar. Part II: Exchange Arrangements of Previously Centrally Planned Economies, by Eduardo Borensztein and Paul R. Masson. 1993.

101. Spain: Converging with the European Community, by Michel Galy, Gonzalo Pastor, and Thierry Pujol. 1993.

100. The Gambia: Economic Adjustment in a Small Open Economy, by Michael T. Hadjimichael, Thomas Rumbaugh, and Eric Verreydt. 1992.

99. Mexico: The Strategy to Achieve Sustained Economic Growth, edited by Claudio Loser and Eliot Kalter. 1992.

98. Albania: From Isolation Toward Reform, by Mario I. Blejer, Mauro Mecagni, Ratna Sahay, Richard Hides, Barry Johnston, Piroska Nagy, and Roy Pepper. 1992.

97. Rules and Discretion in International Economic Policy, by Manuel Guitián. 1992.

96. Policy Issues in the Evolving International Monetary System, by Morris Goldstein, Peter Isard, Paul R. Masson, and Mark P. Taylor. 1992.

95. The Fiscal Dimensions of Adjustment in Low-Income Countries, by Karim Nashashibi, Sanjeev Gupta, Claire Liuksila, Henri Lorie, and Walter Mahler. 1992.

94. Tax Harmonization in the European Community: Policy Issues and Analysis, edited by George Kopits. 1992.

93. Regional Trade Arrangements, by Augusto de la Torre and Margaret R. Kelly. 1992.

92. Stabilization and Structural Reform in the Czech and Slovak Federal Republic: First Stage, by Bijan B. Aghevli, Eduardo Borensztein, and Tessa van der Willigen. 1992.

91. Economic Policies for a New South Africa, edited by Desmond Lachman and Kenneth Bercuson with a staff team comprising Daudi Ballali, Robert Corker, Charalambos Christofides, and James Wein. 1992.

90. The Internationalization of Currencies: An Appraisal of the Japanese Yen, by George S. Tavlas and Yuzuru Ozeki. 1992.

89. The Romanian Economic Reform Program, by Dimitri G. Demekas and Mohsin S. Khan. 1991.

88. Value-Added Tax: Administrative and Policy Issues, edited by Alan A. Tait. 1991.

87. Financial Assistance from Arab Countries and Arab Regional Institutions, by Pierre van den Boogaerde. 1991.

86. Ghana: Adjustment and Growth, 1983–91, by Ishan Kapur, Michael T. Hadjimichael, Paul Hilbers, Jerald Schiff, and Philippe Szymczak. 1991.

85. Thailand: Adjusting to Success—Current Policy Issues, by David Robinson, Yangho Byeon, and Ranjit Teja with Wanda Tseng. 1991.

84. Financial Liberalization, Money Demand, and Monetary Policy in Asian Countries, by Wanda Tseng and Robert Corker. 1991.

83. Economic Reform in Hungary Since 1968, by Anthony R. Boote and Janos Somogyi. 1991.

82. Characteristics of a Successful Exchange Rate System, by Jacob A. Frenkel, Morris Goldstein, and Paul R. Masson. 1991.

81. Currency Convertibility and the Transformation of Centrally Planned Economies, by Joshua E. Greene and Peter Isard. 1991.

80. Domestic Public Debt of Externally Indebted Countries, by Pablo E. Guidotti and Manmohan S. Kumar. 1991.

79. The Mongolian People's Republic: Toward a Market Economy, by Elizabeth Milne, John Leimone, Franek Rozwadowski, and Padej Sukachevin. 1991.

78. Exchange Rate Policy in Developing Countries: Some Analytical Issues, by Bijan B. Aghevli, Mohsin S. Khan, and Peter J. Montiel. 1991.

77. Determinants and Systemic Consequences of International Capital Flows, by Morris Goldstein, Donald J. Mathieson, David Folkerts-Landau, Timothy Lane, J. Saúl Lizondo, and Liliana Rojas-Suárez. 1991.

76. China: Economic Reform and Macroeconomic Management, by Mario Blejer, David Burton, Steven Dunaway, and Gyorgy Szapary. 1991.

75. German Unification: Economic Issues, edited by Leslie Lipschitz and Donogh McDonald. 1990.

74. The Impact of the European Community's Internal Market on the EFTA, by Richard K. Abrams, Peter K. Cornelius, Per L. Hedfors, and Gunnar Tersman. 1990.

73. The European Monetary System: Developments and Perspectives, by Horst Ungerer, Jouko J. Hauvonen, Augusto Lopez-Claros, and Thomas Mayer. 1990.

72. The Czech and Slovak Federal Republic: An Economy in Transition, by Jim Prust and an IMF Staff Team. 1990.

71. MULTIMOD Mark II: A Revised and Extended Model, by Paul Masson, Steven Symansky, and Guy Meredith. 1990.

Note: For information on the title and availability of Occasional Papers not listed, please consult the IMF *Publications Catalog* or contact IMF Publication Services.